Years of PROMISE
1896-1911

Paul W. Bennett

Grolier Limited
TORONTO

CENTURY OF CANADA SERIES

SERIES CONSULTANT: DESMOND MORTON

Dedicated to Kelly Alexandra, and to those of her generation.

Acknowledgements

Many have helped in the preparation of this volume in the Century of Canada Series. Ken Pearson, Vice-President of Grolier, was instrumental in launching and shaping the book and the series. As Series Consultant, Professor Desmond Morton demonstrated his usual high professional standards and offered many valuable comments and suggestions at various stages in its completion. Jocelyn Smyth, the Project Editor, carried out her heavy editing responsibilities with great skill, tact and grace. Two of my colleagues at Upper Canada College deserve special mention: Marian Spence, the U.C.C. Librarian, assisted with the Time Chart and Rick Life developed the sections for Review and Discussion which conclude each chapter. Mere words cannot express my gratitude to my wife Dianne for typing the final drafts and coping with my writing binges. This book is dedicated to our daughter, Kelly. She knows why.

Cover illustrations:

| 1 | 2 | 3 |

1. Sir Wilfrid Laurier.
2. Toronto City Hall, 1910.
3. Pioneering the West.

Illustration credits: Public Archives of Canada, cover (1-C1971) and pages 10 (C5598), 13 (PA17193), 18, 20 (C3775), 23 bottom right (C70870), 27, 28 (C6097), 34 (C4745), 36 (PA33762), 37 (TC744), 39 centre (PA40745), 42 (C63256), 49 (C12035), 67 (PA52774), 69 (PA23636), 80 (PA48475), 81 (C37113), 86 (C28574), 90 (PA73657), 93 (PA122518), 97 (C5480), 98 (C4956), 101 bottom right (C14090), 102 (C4729), 107 (C694); City of Toronto Archives, cover (2) and pages 72, 95, 104, 105; Glenbow Alberta Institute, cover (3) and page 39 (top left and middle right), 100 (middle right); Ontario Archives, pages 16, 52, 62, 63, 83, 100 (bottom left and top right); Metro Toronto Library Board, pages 23, 30, 45, 57; RCMP Archives, pages 24, 59, 60; Saskatoon Public Library, page 39 (top right); Alberta Archives, page 39 (middle left and bottom right); Manitoba Archives, pages 41, 55, 76, 79, 101 (bottom left); Saskatchewan Archives, pages 39 (top left), 44, 65; Ralph Brown, page 47; City of Vancouver Archives, page 58; Nova Scotia Archives, page 100 (bottom right); British Columbia Archives, page 101 (top).

Canadian Cataloguing in Publication Data

Bennett, Paul W., 1949–
  Years of promise, 1896–1911

(Century of Canada series)
Includes index.
ISBN 0-7172-1854-6

1. Canada—History—1867–1914.   2. Canada—Politics and government—1896–1911. *   3. Canada—Social conditions—1867–1918. *
I. Title.   II. Series

FC550.B46 1986   971.05   C86-093554-X
F1033.B46 1986

1234567890 THB 09876

Printed and Bound in Canada

CONTENTS

FOREWORD

There are times in life and history when everything seems hopeless. However hard you try, nothing seems to work. Good advice and bad seem to produce the same disappointing result. Bad luck makes it all seem a little worse. Then, quite suddenly, everything seems to work out. Luck changes. Hard work pays off. Life—and history—looks wonderful again. Indeed, all at once everything seems possible.

In many ways, that is what happened to Canada in 1896. Within a year, a twenty-year economic slump lifted, the last real possibility of a war with the United States vanished and voters chose a brand new government. In a few years, the fruits of the Conservatives' National Policy were harvested by their Liberal opponents. Immigrants poured into Canada, creating markets for booming new industries. Instead of just one transcontinental railway, Sir Wilfrid Laurier's government would soon insist that Canada needed three. Instead of the failure it had seemed to be in the generation after Confederation, Canada was suddenly a brilliant success.

Of course, as Paul Bennett reminds us, good times have problems too. Not everybody shared in the prosperity of Laurier's Canada. Huge fortunes could be made in a time of commercial and industrial expansion but few of the dollars trickled down to the farmers and working people whose hard work made prosperity possible. Much of the wealth was concentrated in Montreal, Toronto, Winnipeg and Vancouver, but so was the poverty, sickness and cruelty of a new industrial age.

Yet remember that it was people in Laurier's era who had the compassion and the opportunity to point out the harsh injustices of the time. Poverty and cruelty were not novelties in Canadian cities nor on the farms and in the mining and logging camps. One of the most exciting features of these years of promise was a new Canadian willingness to recognize social evils and to do something about them.

These are years when women mobilize the arguments and the allies they need to win their fight for political equality. The Laurier years saw Canadian farmers, especially in the West, create the organizations which would eventually help win them political and economic power. Workers, too, built the foundations of a union movement and their own political voice. Other reformers showed that Canadians could rebuild their cities to be clean, safe, comfortable places to live. Governments began to ease away from the corruption and inefficiency of political favouritism. Even businesses discovered the reforming possibilities of efficient management and a commitment to innovation.

All change is accompanied by a recognition of past evils and future possibilities. In these years of promise, prosperity helped give Canadians a vision of how great their country could be.

Probably no period in our history has been more intensively studied than the years from 1896 to 1914. The Laurier years have fascinated historians because so many of the developments that matter in our own time, from American investment to the struggle for women's rights, seem to emerge in this period. Paul Bennett was the ideal person to write of this period. Not only has his own research been focused on the Laurier years, his skill as a synthesizer of masses of material has been demonstrated in several popular textbooks. He brings an impressive record as a classroom teacher to the interpretation of an era of bewildering complexity.

Desmond Morton
University of Toronto

EVENTS 1896–1911

Year	Canada	The World
1896	— Wilfrid Laurier leads the Liberals to victory in a general election. — Gold discovered in the Klondike. — Niagara Falls hydroelectric plant opens. — Clifford Sifton appointed Minister of the Interior, launches campaign to settle the West.	— First modern Olympics held in Greece. — Nobel Prizes are established for achievements in service of mankind. — French physicist Henri Becquerel discovers radioactivity. — William McKinley elected President of the United States.
1897	— Responsible government granted to North-West Territories. — Canada celebrates Queen Victoria's Diamond Jubilee and Prime Minister Laurier is knighted. — First Women's Institute founded at Stoney Creek, Ontario, by Adelaide Hoodless.	— Turkey declares war on Greece. Peace settlement establishes an independent island of Crete. — Colonial Conference at London. — British author Rudyard Kipling publishes *Captains Courageous* and playwright G.B. Shaw produces *Candida*.
1898	— Prohibition triumphs in a Dominion plebiscite. — Gold rush attracts thousands to Klondike and sparks a dispute over Alaska boundary. — The Earl of Minto replaces Lord Aberdeen as Governor General.	— Spanish–American War. — Pierre and Marie Curie discover radium and polonium. — German Ferdinand Von Zeppelin builds first dirigible (airship).
1899	— Prime Minister Laurier calls for voluntary enlistment of troops for Boer War. — Street railway strike in London, Ontario, is quelled by troops.	— South African War begins between Britain and the Boers. — First magnetic recording of sound.
1900	— Sir Wilfrid Laurier and the Liberals are returned to office in a federal election. — Mackenzie King organizes the federal Department of Labour. — Imperial Order Daughters of the Empire started by Montreal's Margaret Murray. — Frontier College founded to carry education to working men in northern communities.	— Boxer Rebellion—international expeditionary force ends Boxer uprising against Europeans in China. — First trial flight of the dirigible *Zeppelin*. — Scientist R.A. Fessenden transmits spoken words by radio waves. — Sigmund Freud publishes *The Interpretation of Dreams*.
1901	— Marconi receives first Trans-Atlantic wireless message at St. John's, Newfoundland. — Robert Borden replaces Charles Tupper as leader of the Conservatives. — The credit union *(caisse populaire)* movement starts in Quebec.	— Queen Victoria dies and is succeeded by her son, Edward VII. — U.S. President McKinley is assassinated and Theodore Roosevelt becomes President. — First British submarine is launched.
1902	— Treaty of Vereeniging ends Boer War and Canadian contingent returns home. — Samuel Gompers's American Federation of Labor becomes a dominant force in the Canadian labour movement. — Canada's first permanent movie house opens in Vancouver.	— British defeat the Boers and Orange Free State becomes a Crown colony. — Triple Alliance between German, Austria-Hungary and Italy is renewed for another six years. — Colonial Conference meets in London.
1903	— Alaska boundary decision favours the American side, ending the Canada–U.S. dispute. — Silver discovered by railway workers near Cobalt touches off a mining boom in northern Ontario. — Henri Bourassa founds *La Ligue nationaliste canadienne*.	— Orville and Wilbur Wright successfully fly a powered airplane at Kitty Hawk, N.C. — Emmeline Pankhurst founds the British National Women's Social and Political Union. — Henry Ford, with $100 000 in capital, starts the Ford Motor Company.

1904 — Klondike Gold Rush in the Yukon comes to an end.
— Charles E. Saunders produces disease-resistant, quick-ripening Marquis wheat.
— Earl Grey succeeds Lord Minto as Governor General.

— France and Britain sign the Entente Cordiale, ending their historic rivalry.
— Russo–Japanese War breaks out in Far East.
— U.S. government launches its anti-trust activities.

1905 — The new provinces of Alberta and Saskatchewan enter Confederation.
— Election of James P. Whitney ends Liberal domination of Ontario politics.
— Laurier and the Liberals win re-election in Ottawa.

— Russo–Japanese War ends with Treaty of Portsmouth favouring Japan.
— Albert Einstein, German physicist, proposes the special theory of relativity.
— Bill Haywood and his followers found the International Workers of the World.

1906 — Ontario Hydro-Electric Power Commission established under Adam Beck.
— Strike in the Alberta coal fields lasts nine months, leaving settlers in danger of freezing.

— First super battleship launched in Britain, the *Dreadnought.*
— Upton Sinclair's novel *The Jungle* reveals the horrors of the Chicago stockyards.
— U.S. passes Pure Food and Drug Act.

1907 — Industrial Disputes Investigation Act, drafted by Mackenzie King, passes into law.
— Anti-Oriental riots erupt in Vancouver.
— Poet Robert Service publishes *Songs of a Sourdough.*

— Panic of 1907 causes a run on the banks before stability restored.
— Lord Baden-Powell founds Boy Scout movement.
— Rudyard Kipling wins Nobel Prize for Literature.

1908 — Laurier and the Liberals win re-election for fourth time.
— Civil Service Commission established for the selection of federal public servants.
— Lucy Maude Montgomery publishes *Anne of Green Gables.*
— Ernest Thompson Seton founds Boy Scouts of Canada.

— Austria annexes Bosnia and Herzegovina and blocks Russian warships from passage through the Dardanelles, threatening war in Balkans.
— Britain passes Old Age Pension Act.
— William H. Taft elected President of the U.S.
— General Motors is formed and the Ford Motor Company produces first "Model T."

1909 — Canadian government creates Department of External Affairs.
— Boundary Waters Treaty signed with the U.S., establishing a permanent International Joint Commission.
— J.A.D. McCurdy makes first airplane flight in Canada at Baddeck, N.S., in *Silver Dart.*

— British Budget of 1909, aimed at aiding the poor, is blocked by the House of Lords.
— Canadian-born actress Mary Pickford emerges as the first film star.
— Imperial Conference on defence.

1910 — Laurier government passes Naval Bill, creating a Canadian navy.
— Combines Investigation Act is passed into law.
— W.S. Fielding negotiates a Reciprocity Agreement with the U.S.

— George V becomes King of Great Britain and Ireland, succeeding his father Edward VII.
— Union of South Africa is established and recognized as a dominion within British Empire.

1911 — Reciprocity Treaty with U.S. is rejected in general election.
— Laurier government defeated after 15 years in power by R.L. Borden and the Conservatives.

— Britain enacts major reforms of Parliament and establishes social security system.
— Germany continues its naval building race with Britain.

INTRODUCTION

At last Canada's hour had struck. The settlement of the western plains had long dragged on with disheartening slowness and eastern development, except for the two or three largest cities, had kept the same pace. Then after 1896 a fortunate combination of circumstances brought a sudden and remarkable change.

O.D. Skelton, Canadian political economist and confidant of Sir Wilfrid Laurier, 1913

Canada's past has its share of myths, and the period from 1896 to 1911 is no exception. It is popularly considered to have been a glorious age of change and progress and is known variously as the Golden Age of Laurier, the Wheat Boom, and the Prosperity Years. Sir Wilfrid Laurier's well-known boast that "the twentieth century belongs to Canada" is closely identified with the buoyant spirit of the times.

Laurier, Canada's prime minister, was described by his friend and biographer, O.D. Skelton, as "the finest and simplest gentleman, the noblest and most unselfish man" of his generation to grace Canadian politics. His popular image was that of Sir Galahad, dressed in shining armour and white plumage, fighting for the cause of Canadian unity. As the country's first French-Canadian prime minister, he seemed to be the living symbol of peace and harmony between French and English Canadians.

The rise of Laurier and his Liberal party to power in 1896 coincided with a revival of world trade and the return of prosperous times after a prolonged depression. The years that followed were a time of amazing economic growth and bright promise for Canada and Canadians. At imperial conferences in 1897 and 1902, a confident Laurier staked Canada's claim as a self-governing Dominion within the British Empire. By the time he and the Liberals met political defeat in 1911, Canada seemed to have been transformed into a modern, industrial, and self-reliant nation.

Between 1896 and 1905, a flood of agricultural settlers, mainly from the United States and Europe, came to Canada's "Last Best West," and two new provinces were created, Alberta and Saskatchewan. Canada's population jumped from just over five million in 1901 to over seven million ten years later. Two new transcontinental railways were built to help carry wheat, known as the gold of the prairie West, eastward for shipment to the bakeries of Europe. Prospering western farmers provided a new market for eastern manufacturers. The northern frontiers of Ontario and Quebec and the British Columbia hinterland opened up, revealing vast new sources of minerals, power and timber.

Over the fifteen years of the Laurier era, Canada seemed on the verge of fulfilling the grand design of Sir John A. Macdonald's National Policy—the creation of a strong, unified national economy. As the West was settled and wheat production mounted, Canada's east-west trading system flourished as never before. The coming of prosperity swept aside many doubts about Canada's future.

Describing Canada during the Laurier years, two British observers in 1905 wrote: "Fate holds in store for this young Dominion a golden future. From whatever point of view we regard it, the Canadian prospect is full of promise. It is safe to say that the natural resources of the country, viewed as a whole, are absolutely unequalled. In her vast forests, her coast and inland fisheries, her exhaustless coal deposits, her gold and silver mines, iron, copper, nickel, and nearly every other known variety of mineral, and, above all, in the tremendous possibilities of her grain fields, Canada holds the promise of such commercial prosperity as the world has seldom seen."

Such are the myths of the Golden Age of Laurier. But what was Canada really like in the boom years from 1896 to 1911? To what extent were Laurier's policies responsible for the tremendous economic expansion? Did his approach to imperial relations always further the cause of Dominion autonomy within the Empire? Did all regions, groups and classes actually share in the prosperity of these years? Was the great promise of the Laurier era ever really fulfilled? This book will explore the Canadian experience in the Laurier era. You are invited to examine some of the myths and realities of life in Canada's "Years of Promise."

1

SUNNY WAYS

The scene was the town hall at Morrisburg, an Ontario hamlet on the shores of the St. Lawrence River. It was the evening of October 8, 1895, and Morrisburg was the first stop on Liberal leader Wilfrid Laurier's Ontario speaking tour.

The crowd was typical of most of this part of conservative, Protestant eastern Ontario. Like the Saturday band concert, fall fair or weekly square dance, the visit of a major public figure was an event. Most of those assembled were dressed according to their station in life. Townsmen appeared stiff and proper in their starched collars, detachable shirt cuffs and bowler hats. A sprinkling of weather-beaten farmers from the surrounding townships were in attendance, looking uncomfortable in store-bought clothes. The few women were swathed in layer on layer of cloth—drawers, corset, petticoat, chemise—all sheathed in dresses which almost brushed the hardwood floors.

Canada was changing, but here the old Victorian values still held sway. The role and importance of the Queen, the Union Jack, duty, honour, virtue and family life were all clearly defined. Protestant attitudes and prejudices towards Catholics and French Canadians, formed in childhood, could last a lifetime. Faith in God, the British Empire and honest toil gave purpose and stability to life.

Wilfrid Laurier and the Sunny Way

On this autumn evening in 1895, Wilfrid Laurier was in the middle of a political crisis. Pressure was mounting on the leader of the federal Liberal party to break his prolonged silence and clarify his position on the most controversial issue of the day, the Manitoba schools question. As a French-Canadian Roman Catholic, he was deeply disturbed over the attempt by the Manitoba government of Thomas Greenway to abolish tax support for separate schools, and he sympathized with the plight of that province's French-Catholic minority. Yet his own party was badly divided on the schools issue. Many of his closest political friends favoured a policy of "provincial rights"; some urged him to steer a middle path, avoid the issue and shift all the responsibility to the floundering Conservative government in Ottawa.

What would Laurier do? Speak out, state his opinions and risk the unity of his party? Or stall for time, hoping that the Tory government would crumble from internal divisions?

Laurier's arrival at the meeting hall charged the room with an air of anticipation. Animated talk among the townsfolk about the divisive schools issue subsided. All eyes were fixed on the French-Catholic Liberal leader as he and his *entourage* strode to the flag-draped platform.

After a formal introduction and hearty applause, Laurier rose to set out his carefully constructed position. With a touch of

Opposite page: Wilfrid Laurier campaigning. "If there is anything to which I have devoted my political life," he once explained, "it is to try to promote unity, harmony and amity between the diverse elements of this country. My friends can desert me, they can remove their confidence from me, they can withdraw the trust they have placed in my hands; but never shall I deviate from that line of policy."

drama, he likened his situation to that of the English military hero, the Duke of Wellington, fighting the armies of Napoleon. Like Wellington at the *Torres Vedras*, he explained, he too had withdrawn behind the battlements and lay waiting for his enemy, the Tory ministry in Ottawa, to take the initiative. With the Tories in disarray, he refused to commit himself to any specific action. Instead he urged an investigation to "get the facts" and cool out the crisis.

The dramatic climax of his speech revealed the guiding principle of an emerging political philosophy. It found its origin in Aesop's fable about the North Wind failing to make a traveller remove his coat—but the sun succeeding. Recalling the fable, Laurier spoke the phrase that came to symbolize his approach to government: "If it were in my power, I would try the sunny way. I would approach this man Greenway with the sunny way of patriotism, asking him to be just and to be fair, asking him to be generous to the minority, in order that we may have peace among all the creeds and races which it has pleased God to bring upon this corner of our common country."

Beneath the dazzling oratory and platform theatrics, Laurier's speech carried an important signal of the practical principle that would guide much of his political career. The politics of the "sunny way" formed the very essence of Laurier liberalism.

The Manitoba Schools Crisis

Why had the dispute over school rights in Manitoba become a full-blown national crisis?

Manitoba's government had sparked the controversy five years earlier by passing legislation that established a single, non-denominational system of tax-supported public schools and by abolishing French as an official language in the province. Both these actions violated guarantees included in the Manitoba Act of 1870. The French-speaking minority in Manitoba urged a succession of federal Conservative governments to disallow the offending legislation. Nothing happened. The predominantly French and Catholic province of Quebec was outraged; Protestant extremists in Ontario insisted ever more loudly on "One Language, One School system in a British Country." Finally, after years of dithering, the Conservative government under Mackenzie Bowell and Charles Tupper went on record as favouring "remedial legislation" to coerce the Manitoba government into revising its troublesome school legislation. Now many Conservatives were outraged.

Amid the swirling controversy of the Manitoba schools question, Laurier smelled the scent of power. The era of Sir John A. Macdonald had come to an end with his death in 1891, and his Conservative successors, four of them in five years, seemed in-

capable of grappling with the schools question. The Conservatives had succeeded only in dividing both their party and the country. Laurier was determined to keep his own party united. If he succeeded, the Tories would defeat themselves and eighteen long years in opposition would be over for the Liberals.

Turn-of-the-century summer fashions on display in Vancouver's Stanley Park.

A Model Leader

The Liberals' first French-Canadian leader seemed admirably suited to the challenge of power in the mid-1890s. Tall and distinguished, with aristocratic features and greying hair sweeping back from his high forehead, Laurier looked the part of a leader. His frock-coated suits, double-breated vests and knotted ascots, his top hat and tails were stylish and elegant. A lawyer by profession and a man of culture, he was renowned for his brilliant oratory and his fluency in both of Canada's official languages. His broad smile and gracious charm won him genuine admiration from political friend and foe alike. Yet beneath the warmth and the charm there lay another Laurier: a masterful politician with the will and determination to keep Canada united and give it a sense of purpose.

Wilfrid Laurier was born and raised in the little Quebec village of Saint-Lin, and educated at the Catholic Collège de l'Assomption and at McGill University's Faculty of Law. As a young lawyer he was sympathetic to the *Rouges*, the French-Canadian radical, anti-clerical party. He was an active opponent of Confederation in the 1860s, but his views gradually moderated as his political ambitions grew.

First elected to the Quebec legislature as the Liberal member for Drummond-Arthabaska in 1871, then to the House of Commons in 1874, Laurier served a long political apprenticeship. For several years he concentrated his energies on overcoming the Quebec Catholic Church's strong opposition to the Liberal party.

He served briefly as a minister in Alexander Mackenzie's Liberal government then faded for a while into relative obscurity when the Conservatives returned to power. In the aftermath of the Northwest Rebellion of 1885, however, he attracted widespread attention with his impassioned pleas for a better understanding between French- and English-speaking Canadians. Throughout the rest of Laurier's political career, this would be his over-riding concern. "My object is to consolidate Confederation," he wrote to a friend some years later, "and to bring our people, long estranged from each other, gradually to become a nation. This is the supreme issue. Everything else is subordinate to that idea."

By the time Laurier succeeded Edward Blake as Liberal leader in 1887, he had learned that a successful politician—like the Old Chieftain, Sir John A. Macdonald—required perseverance, organizing skill, the ability to manage men and, above all, a talent for compromise. To act evasively to defuse divisive issues might not be heroic, but it could preserve unity—and aid in securing and maintaining power.

The Triumph of 1896

By the spring of 1896 a federal election was underway, fought largely on the contentious Manitoba schools issue. Feeling power within his grasp, Laurier continued to steer a middle course between the strongly Protestant elements in English-speaking Canada and the French Catholics of Manitoba who had captured the sympathy of Quebec. In Quebec, he promised to protect the minority in Manitoba through compromise. He asked *Québécois* to trust him, a French Catholic, to find a solution. In Ontario meanwhile, his supporters accused the Conservatives of trying to overrule a province in order to woo the Roman Catholic Church in Quebec.

Laurier's strategy worked. Election day—June 23, 1896—saw the Liberals capture 117 seats to 89 for Tupper's Conservatives. Laurier's own natural appeal carried the day in Quebec, where the Liberals swept 49 of 65 seats. They held their own in Ontario, winning 43 ridings to the Tories 44, and improved their position in most of the rest of the country. The long era of Con-

"And I will say this, that we are all Canadians. Below the island of Montreal the water that comes from the north from Ottawa unites with the waters that come from the western lakes, but uniting they do not mix. There they run parallel, separate, distinguishable, and yet are one stream. . . a perfect image of our nation. We may not assimilate, we may not blend, but for all that we are still the component parts of the same country."

Wilfrid Laurier, speaking in Toronto, December 10, 1886.

servative rule, firmly established by Macdonald and stretching back almost two decades, had come to an end.

The election triumph of 1896 began a heady time for Laurier and the Liberals. A majority of Canadians looked eagerly to the country's first French-Canadian prime minister for the conciliatory and constructive leadership so desperately needed in a period of internal division and economic stagnation. But the lessons of 1896 would not soon be forgotten. Indeed these lessons—the importance of preserving a solid bloc of Quebec support and the need to seek political compromises—would keep Laurier in power for fifteen years.

Laurier and the "Ministry of All Talents"

On the morning of July 11, 1896, Wilfrid Laurier was invited to Government House by Canada's Governor General, Lord Aberdeen. In a brief ceremony amid the regal splendour of Rideau Hall, the Liberal leader was commissioned to form a government and sworn in as Canada's seventh prime minister. At the age of fifty-five, Laurier was at the height of his powers and he brought the promise of new style and grace to the office.

Zoe Laurier, his wife of twenty-six years, approached her new role in official Ottawa with feelings of apprehension. She had never lost her small-town attitudes and enjoyed gardening and entertaining neighbourhood children more than she relished politics or the limelight of power. Laurier's wife never much cared for Ottawa. "Here I belong to everyone and no one in particular," she confessed to a friend. "I would rather be the wife of a simple *avocat* in Arthabaska. It was the best time in my life."

Laurier's new position, however, brought one benefit welcomed by his wife. For the first time in their marriage, they were free of financial worries. The office did not pay well, but Laurier's admirers were generous. After the election a group of supporters offered to raise a fund of between $50 000 and $100 000 for the Lauriers' personal use. It was an offer that Laurier gratefully accepted since there were no strings attached. Nor would the arrangement draw criticism from his opponents: John A. Macdonald had accepted a similar offer to ensure that he could devote his full energies to political life. A jubilant Liberal party provided the Lauriers with its own gift of a very pleasant house in Ottawa, within walking distance of Parliament Hill.

The first challenge to the new prime minister's political skill lay in forming a cabinet. After eighteen years in opposition, this was no easy task. Laurier's own experience in cabinet consisted of scarcely a year in the Mackenzie administration. The only other holdover from that earlier ministry, Sir Richard Cartwright, was regarded with suspicion for his strong advocacy of unrestricted reciprocity in the 1880s and early 1890s.

Sir Charles Tupper was in his mid-seventies when he undertook to rally his dispirited party for the 1896 election. He ran an amazingly vigorous campaign, and although he failed to deliver a victory he may have prevented a rout. Tupper stayed on as leader of the opposition until his defeat in the 1900 general election, when he retired from public life. He died in England in 1915 at the age of ninety-three.

Laurier's fifteen years in power remain the longest unbroken term of office for any Canadian prime minister.

Although the population shift to the cities was well underway by the turn of the century, over 60 percent of Canadians still lived in rural areas and shopped in general stores like this one.

Laurier attempted to build a cabinet which was all things to all people. By the time of his triumph in 1896, he understood the contending forces which characterized Canada, and he sought to recognize each of these forces in his cabinet. From Quebec, he selected a mixture of old *Bleus* like Israel Tarte and reform Liberals closer to his own stripe. With Quebec taken care of, Laurier turned his attention to the rest of the country. He recognized the importance of Canadians' strong identification with their own province or region, and while he sought to instil a strong sense of national purpose, he realized that the way to accomplish this lay in acknowledging regional loyalties. Thus, he brought a group of men with strong provincial backings into his first cabinet.

Laurier's cabinet choices bore testimony to his shrewd political judgement. Oliver Mowat, the aging and popular premier of Ontario, was appointed for his soundness and respectability. W.S. Fielding, premier of Nova Scotia and A.G. Blair, premier of New Brunswick, were selected in an effort to ensure a strong Maritime presence in the cabinet. Clifford Sifton, a youthful Manitoba cabinet minister, was enticed to Ottawa to take charge of western development. English-speaking Protestants in Quebec, Irish Catholics in Ontario, industrialists, bankers and farmers— all were given representatives. It was a remarkable collection of talents. Time would dull their enthusiasm, expose their differences, and even sap their moral strength, but in the exciting days of 1896 it was a team that showed great promise.

A Classic Laurier Compromise

The first task of the new cabinet was to settle the still unresolved Manitoba schools question. During the campaign Laurier had promised "sunny ways"—an approach of gentle persuasion rather than direct federal action. Once in office he treated the dispute with great delicacy. He corresponded diplomatically with Premier Greenway, then dispatched federal emissaries to Winnipeg. Within a matter of months, both sides had agreed upon a compromise settlement which recognized the principle of public, non-denominational schools, yet granted some significant concessions to the French and Catholic minorities.

The Laurier-Greenway settlement of 1897 was a fine example of the art of compromise. Tax support for Catholic separate schools was not restored, but within the Manitoba public school system there could be after-hours Catholic religious instruction and some teaching on a bilingual basis in schools where the numbers of pupils speaking French (or any language other than English) warranted. The settlement fell short of what the Catholics had demanded, but neither was it everything that the Manitoba government and its Orange Protestant supporters in Ontario had been insisting upon for years. Such a compromise pleased no one completely. Many in the West were against permitting linguistic minorities to teach even partly in their own language. They wanted a school system like that of the neighbouring United States which would help to assimilate and "nationalize" minorities.

Nor did the accord satisfy the Catholic bishops. In fact Archbishop L.N. Bégin of Quebec, a respected moderate among the Catholic hierarchy, spoke out furiously against what he called a total abandonment of "the best established and most sacred rights of the Catholic minority." But Laurier brought the bishops to heel by skilful diplomacy with the Vatican in Rome. A round of careful negotiations during 1897 concluded with the issuing of a Papal Encyclical urging Catholics to accept the settlement as the best possible under the existing political circumstances. Most Canadians were relieved to see the nagging issue fade away.

Heir to Sir John, Friend of Business

A key element in Laurier's broadening appeal was his amazing success at wooing and subduing his critics among Canadian business interests. This was a remarkable feat. Canada's industrialists and financiers had always looked to Sir John A. Macdonald's Tories as the party most likely to serve their interests and had viewed the Liberals with suspicion since their flirtation with free trade in the 1880s. But now Laurier enjoyed a measure of acceptance in business circles. Why the turnabout?

Laurier's *rapprochement* with business was typical of his

The bilingual provisions of the 1897 school act were rescinded in 1916. Not until the 1970s would French again be legally permitted as a language of instruction in Manitoba public schools.

"sunny ways" approach. Following the election of 1891, he and other Liberal leaders had decided that support for tariff protection for Canadian industry was essential to their political success. Over the next five years a concerted attempt was made to identify the Liberal party with the gospel of protection so dear to the hearts of Canadian business interests.

The campaign to win business favour reached its climax in the election of 1896. Leading members of the Toronto financial and industrial establishment, as well as Montreal tycoons and entrepreneurs, were either approached and befriended or invited to join Laurier for cozy sessions behind closed doors. "The intention of the Liberal Party," Laurier boldly proclaimed in the Toronto *Globe*, "is not and never was to establish absolute free trade in this country." Laurier's Liberals, the newspaper noted with relish, had recognized that Canadian manufacturers required "stability and permanency" in order to prosper.

Once in office Laurier spared no effort to cement his alliance of convenience with Canada's business community. The announcement that the champion of protectionist Liberalism, Premier Oliver Mowat, would serve in the Laurier cabinet did much to dispel remaining misgivings. The alliance was further solidified by the choice of W.S. Fielding for the finance portfolio (rather than that long-time Liberal advocate of free trade, Sir Richard Cartwright), and by the appointment of a government commission which invited businessmen to participate fully in the process of tariff revision.

A new tariff policy introduced in the Liberal budget of 1897, not only left National Policy protection virtually untouched, but also contained some long-desired provisions for preferential trade with Great Britain. Staunch Conservative protectionists like the former prime minister, Sir Mackenzie Bowell, were left wringing their hands. The new government's economic policies, he snapped sarcastically in the Senate, were those of the "veriest Tories in the land." The business community was delighted.

Laurier, the prime minister of the sunny way, was off to a promising start. The Catholic–Protestant conflict over school rights had been brought under control; businessmen's uncertainties over trade policy had been calmed; and the country showed signs of being ready to turn away from the old divisive issues of the 1880s and early 1890s. The Dominion seemed to be coming of age and starting to fulfil the promise of Confederation.

Yet the country was also entering a new era in its relations with Great Britain and the United States. Maintaining national unity under the changing circumstances would present a severe test of Laurier's leadership.

REVIEW AND DISCUSSION

Note: Many of the "Key People" who are identified in one chapter appear in others as well. Readers should keep track of the ongoing importance of these individuals.

Key People and Ideas
Explain the importance of each of the following as they are discussed in the chapter.

Wilfrid Laurier	Oliver Mowat
Edward Blake	W.S. Fielding
Lord Aberdeen	A.G. Blair
Zoe Laurier	Clifford Sifton
Sir Richard Cartwright	Premier Greenway
Israel Tarte	Archbishop Bégin
	Manitoba Act of 1870

Analysing the Issues
Answer each of the following questions, which deal with important issues raised in the chapter.

1. What were the guiding principles of Wilfrid Laurier's political philosophy?
2. What caused the Manitoba Schools Question?
3. What was the basis of Laurier's settlement of the Manitoba School's Question?
4. What steps did Laurier take to improve the relationship between his Liberal party and the Canadian business community?

Questions for Discussion
Think carefully about each of the following questions and discuss the issues they raise.

1. Why was it necessary for Laurier to accept the protectionist economic policies of the Conservatives during the 1890s? What does this tell you about political power in Canada at the time?
2. Was Laurier's "Sunny Ways" policy of compromise likely to lead to political solutions which were good for Canadians or was it simply a policy which would benefit the Liberal party by keeping it in power?

2

AUTONOMY
WITHIN THE EMPIRE

As the nineteenth century drew to a close, a new idea of "imperialism" was gaining strength. Victoria, Queen of England, reigned over a vast empire that covered one-quarter of the globe. In Britain and in many of her colonies, there was a tremendous feeling of pride in the great, far-flung British Empire. The new imperialists dreamed of reshaping that empire, of unifying the colonies in a single global federation that would link one-fifth of the world's people in a common union of institutions, language and law.

In Canada, nowhere was the spirit of imperial feeling stronger than in the English-speaking public schools. Every Canadian boy and girl in schools throughout the English-speaking parts of the country was taught from texts produced in England or from books slightly modified for Canadian pupils. Empire Day—May 23 of each year, the day before Queen Victoria's birthday—was a big event in the schools. The whole day was devoted to celebrating Canada's place in the Empire. Streets filled with parades of children waving British flags and maple leaves; classrooms rang with the sounds of patriotic poetry and songs; pupils eagerly competed in mammoth essay-writing contests.

The *Ontario Readers* of the late 1890s and early 1900s captured this spirit of British loyalty and carried a strong British-Canadian message. On the flyleaf, beneath the Union Jack, appeared the motto "One Flag, One Fleet, One Throne." Inside the readers, girls and boys were treated to a portrait of the ruling monarch and poetry selections such as Rudyard Kipling's "Oh Motherland, we pledge to thee,/Head, heart and hand through years to be." There were passages from Thomson's "Rule Britannia," Tennyson's "Funeral of Wellington," and verses from W.E. Henley:

> Mother of Ships whose might,
> England, my England,
> Is the fierce old Sea's delight,
> England, my own,
> Chosen daughter of the Lord,
> Spouse-in-Chief of the ancient Sword,
> There's the menace of the Word,
> In the Song on your bugles blown, England—
> Out of Heaven on your bugles blown!

Britain was not alone in trumpeting the gospel of imperialism. Canada's North American neighbour was now a rising world power. At a time when Britain and other European powers were building up empires, the United States began to flex its muscles and sought to assert its national interests. Americans considered it their mission to bring the blessings of their civilization to Latin America and other parts of the world. English-Canadian loyalties and sentiments would be tested in the coming years.

Opposite page:
The Governor General and Lady Aberdeen visit the Lauriers at Arthabaska in 1897. Seated left to right are Sir Wilfrid, Lady Aberdeen, Lord Aberdeen and Lady Laurier.

A New Vision of Empire

When Wilfrid Laurier's government took office in 1896, the style of imperialism was firmly established in London. Gone was the view that had prevailed in the 1860s and 1870s that the Empire was little more than a chain of millstones around Britannia's neck. Leading figures in Britain had come to see the colonies as a source of strength for the mother country. Foremost among the British imperialists were such men as Joseph Chamberlain, the dynamic former businessman who served as Colonial Secretary from 1895 to 1903; Cecil Rhodes, the British-born capitalist and politician who sought to extend British rule in Africa; and Rudyard Kipling, the world-renowned poet.

This new imperialism gave birth to a new, compelling vision of the Empire—the Imperial Federation idea. Speaking in Toronto in 1888, Joseph Chamberlain had captured the nature and spirit of the scheme:

> What is the fact in regard to these peoples, the older and the younger nations? Our past is theirs. Their future is ours. You cannot, if you would, break the invisible bond which binds us together. . . . It may be that the Confederation of Canada may be the lamp lighting our path to the federation of the British Empire. If it is a dream—it may be the imagination of an enthusiast—it is a grand idea. It is one to stimulate the patriotism and statesmanship of every man who loves his country. . . . Let us do all in our power to promote it and enlarge the relations and goodwill which ought always to exist between the sons of England throughout the world and the old folks at home.

Imperialist sentiment did not always take the same form. Leaders of the imperial unity movement like Chamberlain saw the Empire as a bulwark of Britain's power. Social reformers in Britain viewed a thriving overseas empire as an outlet for growing populations and a source of social regeneration, capable of reforming British society. In its extreme variation, the new spirit of imperialism degenerated into jingoism, a crude chest-thumping cry for military conquest and adventurism. Whatever their shape and form, imperialist ideas certainly fueled the European scramble for colonial possessions in Africa, the South African and Spanish-American wars at the turn of the century, and the growing military rivalry between Great Britain and Germany leading up to world war in 1914.

The Canadian Variety of Imperialism

Like Britain, Canada had her imperialists. The spirit of Anglo-Saxon superiority and the sense of mission associated with the call

VOICES AND SYMBOLS
OF CANADIAN IMPERIALISM

One Flag
One Fleet
One Throne

The Union Jack

*Inside front cover of
1910* Ontario Reader.

Front page of the Toronto Globe, *Saturday, November 3, 1900.*

"The watchword now is: Canada, one and inseparable, now and forever, an integral part of the Empire. Let us bear our burdens of the Empire like honourable men, and whenever Britain goes forth to battle, Canada's sons and daughters in their field of duty, will be found standing by the honour of old England."

*Hon. George W. Ross, Premier of Ontario and Vice-President
of the Toronto branch of the British Empire League, September 20, 1900.*

"To many people in Canada this imperialism is a tainted word. It is too much associated with a truckling subservience to English people and English ideas and the silly swagger of the hop-o'-my-thumb junior officer. But there is and must be for the future of our country, a higher and more real imperialism that this—the imperialism of the plain man at the plough and the clerk in the counting house, the imperialism of any decent citizen that demands for this country its proper place in the councils of the Empire and in the destiny of the world. In this sense, imperialism means but the realization of a Greater Canada, the recognition of a wider citizenship.

I . . . am an Imperialist because I will not be a Colonial. . . ."

*Stephen Leacock,
"Greater Canada: An Appeal,"
University Magazine, April 1907.*

"Carry the word to my sisters—
To the Queens of the East and the South
I have proven faith in the Heritage
By more than word of the mouth
They that are wise may follow
Ere the world's war trumpet blows,
But I—I am first in the battle,"
Said our Lady of the Snows.

*Verse from Rudyard Kipling's
"Our Lady of the Snows," as reprinted
in* The Star, *Montreal, April 28, 1897.*

"For home and country let us arm and boldly face the blast."
*From the 1901 hit song,
"Three Cheers for the Flag."*

▶ *Colonel George
T. Denison,
one of the leading
voices of Canadian
imperialism.*

for imperial unity struck a responsive chord in many English Canadians. A Canadian imperialist movement, which had existed since 1867, came to the fore in the late 1880s and early 1890s amid an atmosphere of doom and gloom. Imperialist ideas appeared at a time when economic depression, growing French–English antagonisms and the threat of commercial union with the United States raised fears of Canada's collapse. The three major spokesmen of imperial unity in Canada—Colonel George T. Denison of Toronto, Principal George M. Grant of Queen's University, and Sir George R. Parkin, teacher and writer—began speaking out in defence of Canada, but soon broadened their appeal.

The Canadian imperialists promoted imperial unity as a unique form of Anglo-Canadian nationalism. To men like George M. Grant, British sentiments and customs formed the core of their "nationality," and contributing to the Empire satisfied a strong English-Canadian desire to play a larger role in the world. The British imperial system, according to the leading imperialists, was not simply a route to further dependence, but rather a "vehicle" through which Canada could attain true nationhood. Some strong imperial-nationalists, like Denison and Sam Hughes, carried the argument even further. Within the Empire, they believed, Canadians' superiority as a people might even make them dominant, not only over other colonials but over Englishmen as well.

Imperial unity did not appeal to all Canadians. The most fervent supporters came from Toronto, parts of rural Ontario and

Contingent of North-West Mounted Police at Queen Victoria's Jubilee. This was the first time the familiar broad-brimmed felt hat was worn officially.

the Maritimes. The movement found little favour with farmers and workers. In French Canada it was greeted with indifference or hostility. But even Wilfrid Laurier, Canada's first French-Canadian prime minister, was obliged to respect the strength of imperialist sentiment in Canada.

The Call to a Great Council

Queen Victoria's Diamond Jubilee celebrations, held in July 1897, gave an enormous boost to the imperialist cause. They also provided Wilfrid Laurier with a splendid setting for his debut on the international diplomatic stage.

As the newly elected leader of Britain's senior self-governing Dominion, Laurier was a centre of attention. With his wife at his side, he attended a round of formal banquets; he rode in a carriage in the magnificent Jubilee pageant; he reviewed the mighty British fleet at Spithead; he accepted honourary degrees at Oxford and Cambridge; he was a guest at Windsor Castle and Buckingham Palace; and, kneeling before the Queen, he was made a Knight of the Grand Cross.

The Jubilee was more than just a royal celebration, however. It was the occasion of a major Colonial Conference, one of a series of diplomatic summit meetings at which the leaders of Britain and the Dominions discussed the state of imperial relations. On the agenda for the Conference was Joseph Chamberlain's ambitious plan for imperial reorganization. In fact, much of the attention lavished on Laurier and his fellow colonial leaders was aimed at promoting the Imperial Federation idea.

As Colonial Secretary, Chamberlain had high hopes for the scheme. He proposed a three-pronged program for uniting the Empire more fully. It called for the creation of a "great council of the Empire," to oversee imperial affairs; a free trade arrangement between Britain and the Dominions; and a single imperial navy, paid for by all and established for the defence of the Empire. Chamberlain spoke of a "true partnership," but many of the assembled premiers feared he was proposing a new association dominated and guided by England for its own purposes.

Laurier's "Everlasting No"

Sir Wilfrid Laurier enjoyed the attention and honours he received in London, but he refused to be swayed by them. In response to Chamberlain's appeal, he set out a carefully constructed position. Since his arrival in England he had made several speeches which seemed to endorse the call for closer imperial ties. Now he spoke more ambiguously. The imperial relationship, he explained, did need to be looked at, but the time for change had not arrived. Unmoved by Chamberlain's rhetoric, he supported a resolution declaring that "the present political relations" were "generally satisfactory under the existing condition of things."

For all his seeming ambiguity on the imperial unity scheme, in his own mind Laurier was clear on one point. The pleas of Canadian anti-imperialists and the views of the majority in French Canada would be heeded. No Canadian commitments would be made to the Empire because such commitments might prove unpopular back home.

This became Laurier's consistent position—critics called it his "everlasting no"—throughout a series of colonial conferences held in 1902, 1903 and 1907. He continued to insist, in characteristically discreet fashion, that the existing imperial ties should neither be formalized nor strengthened. Canada's obligations to the Empire must remain undefined, and the extent of Canada's contribution would be determined in Canada, by Canadians and according to Canadian needs. If representation on an imperial council might retard the growth of Canadian autonomy, Laurier told a group of British businessmen, then he "would have none of it." Canadians would do their part to strengthen the Empire by strengthening the Dominion itself, by making it prosperous, by promoting internal harmony, by developing its resources and potential.

The Boer War Crisis

Laurier's position on imperial unity and his talent for political compromise were soon tested. In early October 1899, Britain found itself on the verge of going to war against the Boers in South Africa, ostensibly to protect the interests of the British colonialists, known as Uitlanders (foreigners), living there. The British Colonial Office issued a request for Canadian military units to fight alongside the British in defence of the Empire.

Britain's request created grave problems for Laurier and his cabinet. Canadian opinion was sharply divided over participation in the South African war. Most English-speaking Canadians, spurred on by staunch imperialists and by the cries of segments of the English-language press, reacted to Britain's call for Canadian troops with enthusiasm. It seemed to be a perfect opportunity to demonstrate the unity and strength of the Empire. Here also was a chance to show Canada's maturity and to aid Britain in her hour of need.

French Canadians saw the conflict in South Africa differently. The French-language press viewed it as an example of British imperial aggression. To many anti-imperialists, it was colonialist Britain's problem and had nothing to do with Canada. While most English Canadians sympathized with the Uitlanders' demand for political rights and admired their champion, Cecil Rhodes, most French Canadians seemed to look upon the issue with profound indifference.

At first Laurier did his best to side-step the issue, hoping that perhaps it might never come to actual war. Joseph Chamberlain's cable of October 3 offering to maintain Canadian troops in South Africa stirred up a hornet's nest. A plan to send a Canadian force, drafted by General Edward Hutton, the British commander of the Canadian Militia, was leaked in the *Canadian Military Gazette*. Laurier dismissed the report of the plan as "pure invention," and continued to straddle the fence, expressing heartfelt support for Britain and claiming that it was up to Parliament to decide on any official action. Meanwhile, the English-Canadian press was howling for action. The shrill *Montreal Star*, published by the flamboyant Hugh Graham, led the way. War hysteria was stirred up by stories condemning the "cowards" in Ottawa for their spineless delays while trainloads of English women and children were being "butchered by the savage Boers."

The Boer War not only brought imperial sentiment to a fever pitch, it also galvanized anti-imperialists into action. They found their strongest base of support in French Canada, and their cause came to be symbolized by one man—Henri Bourassa. Bourassa, a young Quebec M.P. and the grandson of Louis-Joseph Papineau, spearheaded opposition to Canadian participation in what he considered to be an imperialist war. To Bourassa and his supporters, sending troops to South Africa would set a dangerous precedent, leading to further demands for contributions to the defence of the Empire.

At the centre of the controversy over the Boer War was Lord Minto, Canada's Governor General from 1898 to 1904. Many observers, including the influential Liberal journalist John W. Dafoe, saw Minto as a "heavy dragoon" who had been sent to Canada in 1898 to push Chamberlain's imperial policies by every means in his power. Some charged that the Canadian viceroy acted like an "Imperial Commissioner" riding roughshod over Canadian autonomy and conspiring to force Canadian participation in the South African war.

Lord Minto certainly pressed Laurier to make a contribution in keeping with "the importance of Canada." But Minto himself took no responsibility for influencing the government's decision. "I have carefully avoided any appearance of pressing for troops," he reported to Chamberlain, "but I have put what I believe to be the Imperial view of the question strongly before Sir Wilfrid." In fact, Minto's papers reveal his dismay at Laurier's lukewarm reaction to the request for troops. On the eve of the decision, the Governor General concluded that the situation was hopeless and no offer would be made.

One of the nastier interpretations of Laurier's Boer War policy.

The Boer War Compromise

On October 12, Laurier returned to Ottawa from a trip to Chicago to find the country in a state of turmoil and his cabinet in a state of crisis. Britain had declared war on the Boer republics and a decision on Canadian participation could no longer be avoided.

Laurier again found himself caught in the middle, fighting even his own feelings. Like his French-Canadian compatriot Bourassa, he supported Canadian autonomy. He, too, felt somewhat indifferent to the war in far-off South Africa. He, too, resented the interference of General Hutton and the pressure from Lord Minto. For political reasons, however, he was not free to parade his feelings openly. A rising tide of imperial sentiment in Ontario threatened to tear apart the Liberal party and the nation.

After a two-day cabinet crisis, a compromise emerged. The government would equip and send overseas the 2nd (Special Service) Battalion of the Royal Canadian Regiment, numbering over a thousand and commanded by Lieutenant-Colonel William Otter. Once in South Africa, British authorities would finance the operation. One stipulation was that the Canadian contingent would serve as a unit on the battlefield. This was not what the British wanted, but it nonetheless set a precedent for Canadian military participation in future wars.

Laurier's stance was politically shrewd. In his home province of Quebec, he stressed that participation was voluntary and that the contribution was small, and he insisted that this action would not imply any commitment in the future. In Ontario and other centres of imperial sentiment, he posed as a true imperial statesman who had responded to Britain's needs.

Canadian troops at the field hospital at Paardeburg Drift on February 19, 1900. On February 18, the first day of a week-long battle, the Canadians had suffered 82 casualties.

A Parting of the Ways

Like most compromises, the Boer War decision failed to satisfy everyone. Laurier was criticized by some English-Canadian nationalists for not insisting upon independent Canadian participation. Ardent imperialists accused him of not doing enough and letting Britain down; their anti-imperialist counterparts objected to Canada making any contribution at all. Henri Bourassa, who had been an early Laurier supporter, broke with him on the issue. "To govern," he snapped angrily, "is to have courage, to risk power to save a principle."

The first Canadian volunteer force of 1150 men, was quickly dispatched to South Africa. Early the following year, a second official contingent was sent, and other military units, including the mounted regiment known as Lord Strathcona's Horse, were privately raised, financed and sent to fight for the British cause. By war's end some 7000 Canadians had served against the Boers, and most returned home full of colourful tales about the glories of war.

While the war raged in South Africa, a political battle was in progress at home. A week after Laurier's decision to send troops to South Africa, Henri Bourassa resigned his seat in the House of Commons in protest. In the election of 1900, the Boer War was the predominant issue. Bourassa ran in Quebec as an Independent on an anti-imperialist platform. In an attempt to appease both Bourassa and Quebec, Laurier did not run a Liberal against him and he was re-elected unopposed. But the seeds had been planted for future political conflict between Laurier and Bourassa over the question of imperialism.

Tory Ontario and Liberal Quebec

Appeasement was the guiding principle behind the prime minister's tactics during the 1900 election campaign. As Liberal leader, he took the high road—insisting that he had compromised in the interest of national unity and ignoring the taunts of the Tory chief, Sir Charles Tupper, and the wild accusations of the English-Canadian press. He toured Ontario in a private railway car with velvet draperies, ornate scrollwork and crystal chandeliers, stopping to make impassioned appeals for unity on crowded Grand Trunk railway platforms. His silver-tongued oratory made compromise sound honourable.

Laurier's national unity campaign was only a partial success. The number of seats won by the Liberals grew a little in the Maritimes and the West and increased in Quebec—despite Bourassa's anti-imperialist agitation—from 49 in 1896 to 56 in 1900. Only Ontario voters appeared dissatisfied. There, the Liberals lost 8 seats. Overall Liberal strength grew in the House of Commons, from 117 in 1896 to 128 in 1900. Still, some observers saw the elec-

Casualties
Eighty-eight Canadians died in action and 252 were wounded. The Canadian troops suffered severely from disease, however, and a further 136 died of illness or accident.

Georgina Pope
Four Canadian nurses accompanied Colonel Otter's contingent and several more followed later. Georgina Pope, the senior nursing sister, was awarded the Royal Red Cross for conspicuous service in the field. She was the first Canadian ever to receive this honour.

tion results as showing voters in Ontario and Quebec dividing on English-French lines. The "spectacle" of a Liberal Quebec, the *Ottawa Evening Journal* aptly observed, was "due chiefly to the tactics of some crazy Conservatives in Ontario who have Francophobia on the brain."

Canadian–American Relations

Relations with Great Britain were not the only concern of Laurier and his government. Good relations with the United States were obviously desirable, but that country's notion of its "Manifest Destiny" to expand at will over the entire continent had to be kept under close watch. For many Canadians, an emerging sense of nationality rested on a defence of the British connection and a fear of the real or imagined threat of absorption by the rising American empire. The root of Canadian feelings of unease and distrust, according to Lord Minto, lay in the "constant Yankee bluff and swagger" and a suspicion that the American "means to possess Canada for himself."

In the opening years of the Laurier era, Canada's relations with her North American neighbour turned mostly on economic matters. The Canadian tariff, introduced in April 1897 by the Minister of Finance, W.S. Fielding, was more than a partial trade concession to Canadian manufacturers and to imperial sentiment in Britain and Canada; it was partly a retaliatory measure against new high tariffs imposed by the United States. Indeed, Fielding blamed unsatisfactory trade relations between Canada and the United States entirely on the so-called Dingley tariff, claiming that Canada was compelled by American trade policy to impose an equally protectionist schedule of customs duties.

The tariff dispute awakened Laurier and his cabinet to the fact that Canada's relations with its neighbour were in bad repair. In the fall of 1897, Laurier and fisheries minister Sir Louis Davies slipped off to Washington to mend the fences. Laurier's proposal for the appointment of an Anglo-American joint commission to improve relations between Canada and the United States was initially rebuffed. Some months later, however, the Americans reconsidered their position. In March of 1898, with his country on the verge of war with Spain and left with no reliable ally except Great Britain, President William McKinley embraced the idea and a Joint High Commission was established. Laurier and his cabinet hoped the new tribunal would provide a means for settling long-standing disputes over the American tariff, the inshore Atlantic fisheries and the American law barring "alien" Canadian labour. To the Americans, it was seen more as a new tool for promoting Anglo-American friendship.

The Alaska Boundary Question

Any dreams of conflict-free Canadian–American co-operation

Lord Baden-Powell, one of the heroes of the Boer War, founded the Boy Scout movement in 1908.

were quickly dispelled. Within months of the establishment of the Joint High Commission, a serious dispute over the Alaska boundary forced its way onto the agenda. This problem, the last of the serious North American boundary disputes, reached its climax in 1903, but its origins lay in the past.

At issue was the boundary between Canada and Alaska in the so-called Panhandle, which stretches for almost a thousand kilometres down the west coast beside the Yukon and British Columbia. The boundary had been only vaguely set in 1825 in a treaty between Russia, then the owner of Alaska, and Great Britain. In 1867 the United States had purchased Alaska from Russia for seven million dollars, but the Americans had felt no need to clarify the boundary provisions of 1825.

The exact location of the Alaska boundary became an urgent question in the late 1890s when gold was discovered in the Klondike region of Canada's Yukon. With the sudden rush of thousands of prospectors to the Klondike, a lucrative supply trade developed, and Canadian and American interests on the Pacific coast struggled to control it. The rich gold fields were clearly in Canadian territory, but the Americans claimed ownership of all the Pacific coast inlets leading to them. The American claim would leave Canada without reasonably convenient access to the Yukon.

American President Theodore (Teddy) Roosevelt, who took office after McKinley's assassination in 1901, adopted a tough stance. Roosevelt was a firm believer in the policy of "walking quietly but carrying a big stick." Once having identified what American interests were in a region, he was usually ready to employ force to protect them. The United States had annexed Hawaii in 1898 and had taken the Philippines as a prize in the Spanish-American war in 1899. Roosevelt had helped stage a revolution in Panama and was busy imposing a treaty to build a canal there. American intervention in the affairs of nearby states raised fears in Ottawa. For the moment American assertiveness was being directed towards Latin America, but would Canada's turn be next?

Roosevelt proceeded with great vigour to persuade Britain to let the United States have its way in the Alaska boundary dispute. In January 1903, the dispute was referred to a joint commission of six officials, three from the United States and three appointed by Great Britain. Although the arbitration agreement stipulated that each side would appoint "impartial jurists of repute," Roosevelt named his Secretary of War and two senators well known for their hard-line nationalist positions on the Alaska question. The British government named two equally partisan Canadians to the tribunal; the third British appointee was the Lord Chief Justice of England, Lord Alverstone.

Not content with packing the court, Roosevelt sent instructions to the three American commissioners, reminding them that there would "of course be no compromise." He also warned the British privately that if the tribunal failed to uphold the American claim, he would send the marines to "run the line."

As the only truly independent member of the tribunal, Lord Alverstone was in a difficult position. If he agreed with the American demands, he would anger the Laurier government at a time when Britain, and especially Joseph Chamberlain, wanted Canadian co-operation in strengthening the bonds of imperial unity. If he sided with the Canadians, he ran the risk of offending the United States just when many other leading nations were hostile towards Britain over its treatment of the Boers. In the end, Alverstone ruled that the Anglo-Canadian case was feeble and gave the United States almost all it had demanded.

Although the decision was both sound in law and politically sensible, Canadians reacted with an outpouring of bitterness. The two Canadian commissioners, Sir Louis Jetté and Allan Aylesworth, publicly denounced the award as a "sacrifice of the interests of Canada." The Liberal Toronto *Globe* stressed that "resentment is deep and settled. If the least backbone had been exhibited by the British Foreign Office the United States would have had to consent to real arbitration." Newspaper editorials claimed that Canada had been "led like a lamb to slaughter," and one warned darkly that "Canadian independence may eventually be arbitrated away." In the city of Vancouver a theatre crowd was so incensed by the tribunal's decision that it booed lustily when "God Save the King" was played.

Birth Pangs of Autonomy

The Alaska boundary decision had lasting consequences. On the whole, Canadians were less concerned about losing the Panhandle than about the strong-arm tactics the Americans had used to get it. Feelings of anti-Americanism had welled up which would leave a residue of distrust, as Laurier was to discover in the election of 1911. Prominent Canadians like Clifford Sifton recognized that Canadian interests were less important to Britain than good relations with the United States. Many shared Laurier's view that Canada could look after its own welfare only if it obtained the power to conduct its own foreign affairs.

The Alaska boundary dispute thus gave a great stimulus to Canadians' desire for autonomy. Since Canadians could no longer depend on Britain to safeguard their interests, Laurier pointed out, more extensive powers of self-government were necessary. Out of this realization eventually sprang the Department of External Affairs and the permanent International Joint Commission, two initial steps on the long road to full Canadian autonomy.

The anger in Canada over the Alaska dispute soon subsided, but memories lingered. Canadians would henceforth be conscious of the precariousness of their position in the so-called North Atlantic triangle and wary of having their country's national interests sacrificed on the altar of Anglo-American friendship. A French writer, André Siegfried, visiting Canada about this time offered an astute assessment. "After seven years of vague imperialism," he observed, "we find a colony essentially loyal, essentially British, but passionately jealous of her liberties, and quite determined not to yield into any other hands whatsoever the least particle of her autonomy."

This attitude was only partly the result of Canada's troubled relations with its senior partners in the North Atlantic triangle. Partly it was due to the fact that Canada had entered an era of booming prosperity. The nation was bursting at the seams with new-found pride and optimism—and modern Canada was beginning to take shape.

REVIEW AND DISCUSSION

Key People and Ideas
Explain the importance of each of the following as they are discussed in the chapter.

Joseph Chamberlain   Theodore Roosevelt
George T. Denison   Lord Alverstone
George M. Grant
Georgina Pope   Imperialism
Henri Bourassa   Queen Victoria's Diamond Jubilee
Lord Minto   Manifest Destiny

Analysing the Issues
Answer each of the following questions, which deal with important issues raised in the chapter.

1. What were the main similarities and differences in the views of British and Canadian imperialists?
2. How did Laurier respond to Joseph Chamberlain's proposal of Imperial Federation?
3. What was Laurier's solution to the Boer War crisis?
4. How were Canadian attitudes affected by the settlement of the Alaska Boundary Dispute?

Questions for Discussion
Think carefully about each of the following questions and discuss the issues they raise.

1. Although the modern impression of "imperialism" is negative, at the turn of the century it was generally well regarded. How would you account for this change in attitude?
2. Some Canadians regard Canada as playing a "lynch pin" role between Britain and the United States. Others regard Canada as a minor player in this North Atlantic triangle whose interests are often overlooked. Which position do you support? Explain why.

3

THE LAST BEST WEST

"As the nineteenth century was that of the United States, so, I think, the twentieth century shall be filled by Canada." When Sir Wilfrid Laurier spoke these words in January 1904, the luncheon audience at the Canadian Club in Ottawa nodded its approval. He was speaking for a nation buoyant with optimism about its future. Wheat sales were booming, a new phase of railway building was underway, and thousands of settlers were at last pouring into the Canadian prairies, known as "the last best West."

In those bold and confident years, forecasting Canada's population growth was a favourite pastime. Fifty million people by 1950, boasted Laurier. At least eighty million by the end of the century, predicted Lord Strathcona, a founder of the Canadian Pacific Railway. Topping both these claims was a Department of the Interior pamphlet of the time which proclaimed: "There is room for one hundred million, and resources are so great that no one can say how large the population will be fifty years hence."

Any number seemed possible in the boom years. Canada found itself swept along with the tide of a world-wide economic upswing. The industrialization of Europe and the growth of a new class of European city dwellers had created an unprecedented demand for agricultural produce, and especially for wheat. Stimulated by new dry-farming techniques and the development of faster-maturing wheat strains, the boom in the wheat economy of the prairie West was amazing. In 1896, Canadian wheat production totalled a mere 8 million bushels (280 million l). By 1901, the figure was 56 million and a decade later it was 231 million. At first the seemingly limitless prospects for selling wheat had sent settlers flocking to the American midwest, with its milder climate, but soon the good farmland there was all taken. At last the time was ripe for the development of the vast Canadian prairies.

Like a great wave, the immigrants came—from Great Britain, from all parts of Europe and eventually from the United States. Canada's population, which had increased by 24 percent between 1881 and 1901, jumped by a remarkable 34 percent over the next decade. In 1896, the country had five million people; by 1911 it had seven million.

The Young Napoleon
The man who best symbolized the expansionist impulse of the Laurier years was Clifford Sifton, Canada's Minister of the Interior. A Manitoba businessman and lawyer in his mid-thirties, descended from Irish immigrant stock, Sifton possessed an almost unbounded confidence in the potential of the Canadian West. He was ambitious and hard-driving, a man of action, not just words.

Sifton's views on settling the empty lands of western Canada were not expressed in the form of a romantic, nineteenth-century American-type vision linking immigration with freedom and op-

Opposite page: Galician family at the Quebec immigration sheds.

portunity for the world's oppressed. Instead he saw the peopling of the West as part of a practical scheme of economic development which included an expanded national transportation system, the exploitation of natural resources and the development of central Canadian manufacturing. "The place to which our merchants and manufacturers of eastern Canada must look for enlarged markets is Manitoba and the North-West Territories," Sifton boldly asserted. "There will be no markets there until we have the population." The goal of immigration policy was to settle the West as quickly as possible.

On becoming Minister of the Interior in 1896, Sifton persuaded the cabinet that immigration should get top priority. Then he turned at once to the task of transforming a stagnant Immigration Branch into one of the most dynamic agencies of government. Officials were fired, juggled or replaced; Dominion regulations for granting homesteads were simplified; and the CPR was cajoled into specifying its land claims, thus identifying the territory available for free homesteads on the western prairies. Almost overnight the department became aggressive and businesslike, stamped with the personality of the man known to his critics as "the young Napoleon."

With the full backing of the prime minister, the Immigration Branch's budget rose from $900 000 in 1896 to over $4 million in 1905, Sifton's last year as minister. Much of the budget was spent on what Sifton termed the "hard sell"—advertising Canada abroad. "In my judgement," he told the House of Commons in 1899, "the immigration work has to be carried on in the same manner as the sale of any commodity; just as soon as you stop advertising and missionary work the movement is going to stop."

Sifton and his hand-picked team of officials left no doubt about the kind of settlers they were seeking for the Canadian West. Agents were instructed to discourage "labouring men" and "mechanics," unless they met specific needs in the Canadian labour force. The most desirable immigrants were those with agricultural skills and some financial assets from Great Britain, the United States and western Europe. A limited number of poor farmers from eastern Europe were also to be encouraged, just enough to provide a reliable labour pool for economically self-sufficient homesteaders in the West.

But, above all, Sifton was seeking results in his immigration policy. When his ideal settlers failed to arrive in sufficient numbers, he encouraged greater recruiting efforts among central and eastern European peasants eager to escape the pressures of overpopulation and political or religious persecution. Time proved them to be hardy, hard-working and successful agriculturalists, and Sifton would later boast about his role in acquiring the

Clifford Sifton. As Minister of the Interior from 1896 to 1905, Sifton was the chief architect of the immigration policies that brought hundreds of thousands of immigrants to the Canadian West.

thousands of "men in sheepskin coats" living in scattered settlements throughout the West.

Sifton's drive to attract settlers from continental Europe was ingenious—and controversial. Most European nations wanted to keep their people, and they were hostile to immigration agents; some, such as Germany, banned their activities outright. To overcome these obstacles, Sifton and the Interior Department resorted to unorthodox, covert measures. An organization known as the North Atlantic Trading Company was formed in late 1899 with the co-operation of a group of German shipping lines. Operating as discreetly as an espionage ring, the company solicited and screened likely immigrants to Canada from all over continental Europe, from Finland to northern Italy and east to the Slavic states of the Austro-Hungarian Empire. Thousands of "Western Canada" advertisements were translated into a dozen languages, printed on small cards and enclosed in plain envelopes, and distributed quietly through the mails. Agents in Europe and Britain were paid a bonus of five dollars per head for farmers, farm labourers and domestic servants, and two dollars a head for dependent children.

There were those who criticized the North Atlantic Trading Company for its secretive operations and bonus policies. Sifton dismissed them as obstructionists. How immigrants were obtained was only of limited concern to the Minister of the Interior. "Getting results" was what counted. Legal or otherwise, the activities of the North Atlantic Trading Company provided the means of competing with countries like Brazil and Argentina in the race for agricultural settlers.

Plugging the Leak

The results of Sifton's immigration campaign over the first five years were disappointing. By 1901 thousands of immigrants from continental Europe had been transported by colonist cars to the prairies, and over 86 000 Americans had migrated northward to take up free homesteads. Yet the Dominion census of 1901 came as a shock. Canada's population totalled 5 371 000, a net gain of only a half-million people in ten years—an increase no better than that of the depression-plagued 1880s. Canada, it seemed was serving mainly as a stopover point. As fast as immigrants were brought in, Sifton concluded, others left for the more developed and hospitable land to the south. Few countries had ever experienced such a "leakage" of people to a neighbouring nation.

To stem the outflow of immigrants to the American midwest, Clifford Sifton and the Interior Department stepped up their campaign for settlers, particularly in the United States. Millions of maps and illustrated brochures were circulated through agents in eighteen American cities. Advertisements were

Sifton's Interior Department was turned into a virtual propaganda mill. Two million copies of 23 different pamphlets in a variety of languages were produced in 1902, four and a half million in 1906. Each of the pamphlets painted a glowing picture of a vast democratic Dominion, complete with summer sunshine, boundless natural resources and "FREE FARMS FOR THE MILLIONS."

Dutch-language immigration poster.

placed in some 8000 farm newspapers and lecturers were dispatched to "talk up" the "land of promise." The American novelist James Oliver Curwood, who worked with Sifton for two years, called the campaign a "fight for people" conducted with "as much strategy and thought as though an actual war were being waged."

Eventually the tide turned and the inflow of Americans quickened. Rising land prices in the American West convinced many farm labourers, tenants and even farm owners to look to the Canadian Northwest. Sifton's aggressive recruitment drive and the work of several private, American-owned colonization companies seemed to tip the scales. In 1900, only 19 000 settlers moved into Canada from the United States; five years later the number arriving yearly had increased to 58 000, and in 1912-13 some 139 000 Americans flowed in.

The Promised Land

To land-hungry farmers in the American midwest and poor peasants in central and eastern Europe, western Canada did indeed seem like a promised land. Immigration officials in the United States and agents of the North Atlantic Trading Company in continental Europe both preached the same message: free land was available in abundance—sixty-five hectares for every homesteader. For the cost of an overland wagon ride or a steamship ticket and a rail trip to Winnipeg, Canada offered a new beginning. To some eastern Europeans, like the Ukrainian peasants of Galicia in the Austro-Hungarian Empire and religious minorities in Czarist Russia, the West was billed as a gateway to political freedom. Emigration would mean no more heavy taxes to the local landlord, an end to overcrowding of small plots of land, to church tithes and to compulsory military service.

These promises brought thousands of migrants flooding out of their homelands. American frontier farmers poured over the border by rail and by wagon-train. From Britain and all parts of Europe, the discontented, the adventure-seekers and the oppressed flocked to Canadian immigration offices. Sifton's shipping and immigration agents screened them, crammed them into the steerage of ocean liners, and disgorged them like cattle at Halifax and Quebec. In wooden colonist rail cars equipped with cook-stoves, they were shipped across the Dominion and dumped out at various stops on the flat, near-treeless, slough-pitted prairie.

The Sodbusters—Breaking the Ground

Officials from the Department of the Interior's Immigration Branch often helped immigrants to locate their homesteads and sometimes provided those in need of money with the names of local established farmers looking for hired help. But for the most part the settlers were left to fend for themselves. The govern-

ment's official attitude to the newcomers was best summed up by Sifton. "I am not much inclined to granting immigrants special favours," he stated. "Once a man becomes a ward of government, he seems to acquire the sentiments of a pauper and forever after will not stand on his own feet or try to help himself."

Conditions were tough for the first wave of land-hungry sodbusters. Those with money could buy a wagon and a horse; others walked for days to reach their free homestead lands. The earliest pioneers cut the sod and piled it to make the walls of a first small house. The deep, untouched sod, dense with the roots of tough prairie grass, was broken with a single-furrow plough pulled by oxen or even sometimes by teams of straining human beings. Men in the family often trekked to the nearest town to take jobs laying train tracks to earn money for food, coal, a gun, an axe and proper tools. Homesteaders and their families suffered through winter blizzards, grasshopper plagues, and grassfires that could spread incredibly fast. An "oldtimer" in the early years on the western prairie was one who had lasted a year. It took back-breaking work, faith and a measure of luck to survive.

Even wheat-growing was a gamble on the land billed as the "World's Bread Basket." Sawflies could cut the crop like a scythe. Hail storms could flatten a wheat field in the middle of the summer season. Drought could shrivel a crop, rust could blight it, frost could destroy it. But one good crop, even threshed with a wooden flail, called a "poverty stick," could buy horses and machinery—and provide the margin of production that would in time spell success.

"I'll never forget the desolate feeling that came over me," recalled one woman, "when we sat on a box and looked around, not a sign of any other human habitation . . . nothing but bluff and water and grass. Then I realized that . . . if we wanted a house to cover us, a stable for our horses, a well for drinking water, it would all have to be the work of our own hands."

Women of the West

Not all the pioneers on the empty lands of the newly opened West were men. Many women came to the new homesteads with their husbands, brothers or fathers. Many others followed as soon as their men found land. And a few women, who were considered very brave, ventured into the West alone to find work as teachers, domestics or nurses. The women, like their men, endured long and uncomfortable journeys to reach the new land. Often they travelled on their own, or coped with the burden of small children.

First impressions cannot have been pleasant for women from tranquil England or even the well-settled American midwest. The land was raw and the housing—often just a sod or wooden shack—made housekeeping very difficult indeed. Water and fuel were often in short supply. The nearest source for essentials like flour and sugar could be many kilometres away. Winters were cruelly cold and neighbours were few and far between. Many of the West's women pioneers later spoke of loneliness as the greatest hardship they endured in their early years on the prairies.

While the men broke or cleared the land and put in the crops, the women ran households, raised children, created gardens and tended chickens, cows and pigs. A few precious possessions they had brought with them—a lace tablecloth, a set of bone china dishes, or even a fine mahogany sideboard—helped them add cheer to a sod hut or a tiny shack. At the busiest times they often helped in the fields, and if money was really short and the men had to work elsewhere for wages, they might be left to shoulder the entire burden of farm and family alone for months on end. Despite such hardships and the seemingly endless toil, pioneer women found time to support churches and schools. They were helping to create more than new farms on the prairies; they were creating a new society too.

A few prairie women cast aside their traditional role to struggle for public recognition and women's rights. Cora Hind, a talented newspaper reporter who had moved to the West in the 1880s, emerged in the early 1900s as the Manitoba *Free Press* agricultural editor. She became internationally recognized as a leading authority on grain, livestock and dairy conditions and prices. One enterprising English gentlewoman, Georgina Binnie-Clark, established her own wheat farm in the Qu'Appelle Valley in 1906 and sparked, through her example, a spirited "homesteads-for-women" campaign in the western press.

Every year for twenty-five years, Cora Hind spent weeks travelling across the West by train or buggy or on horseback, studying conditions and providing amazingly accurate predictions of crop yields.

These were but the early signs of what would soon become a vigorous—and successful—movement for women's suffrage. Prairie women had made nonsense of arguments that women were "fair, frail flowers" whose constitutions would not stand up to the excitement of elections. When they demanded political equality, the main farmers' newspaper, the *Grain Growers' Guide*, acknowledged them as "fellow partners . . . in the arduous work of making homes on the prairies" and supported their campaign. The majority of western men agreed, and in 1916 the prairie provinces were the first governments in Canada to give women the vote.

The Land of the Second Chance
Not all Canadians were happy about the success of Clifford Sifton's immigration policies. The growing influx of Americans from Nebraska, Minnesota, Iowa and other midwestern states raised the spectre of an "American invasion" of the Canadian West. The Toronto *World* sounded the alarm in 1902: "Americans are pouring into the West by tens of thousands, are buying land through companies and agents in thousands of acres a day, and are preparing to control the factories and trade of the whole region as well as the stock of the Canadian Pacific Railway." A prominent British newspaper correspondent went even further, warning his readers that if Britain stood idly by, the next genera-

Advertising Canadian
prosperity in Exeter,
England.

tion in this part of the Empire would "sing more 'Yankee Doodle' than 'God Save the King'."

Growing fears of this sort and British imperial sentiment did much to awaken the United Kingdom to the possibilities of the Canadian Northwest. A desire to strengthen the ties of Empire, hostility towards the "Yankees" and hard-headed business considerations all figured in the mounting of a mammoth effort to persuade more people of British origin to migrate to western Canada. Feature articles in the popular British press echoed the sentiments expressed in the *Fortnightly Review*, which cautioned: "We must not sit back any longer and watch one of the most promising daughter lands being peopled by settlers of alien blood."

Emigrants from Britain, escaping from the overcrowded labour market and crushing urban poverty of England, had been swelling the American population for many years. Over two-thirds of the 200 000 emigrants who annually left the British Isles joined the throngs from the continent seeking a better life in the United States. Now, because of the interest stirred up in Britain, many began to choose destinations in the "British" Canadian Northwest. By 1905, for the first time in over fifty years, more Britons were coming to Canada than were going to the United States. Although Irish emigration remained small, English and Scots arrived at the Atlantic ports of Canada in numbers greater than those of American settlers coming up from the south.

British immigrants, whether they came directly from the "Old Country" or were enticed away from the United States and from Ontario, were readily absorbed into the emerging pioneer society of western Canada. Settlers of English, Scottish and Irish origin had no language barrier to overcome. For the most part the institutions, traditions and values that existed in Canada were familiar to them, and many quickly moved into positions of prominence in local politics and in farm and labour organizations.

One spectacular exception to the generally smooth settling in of British immigrants was the Barr Colony, promoted by Reverend Isaac Barr in 1903. Almost two thousand Britons, attracted by extravagant promises and patriotic appeals to "save Canada for the British Empire" set out for Barr's chosen site near Lloydminister, Saskatchewan. Unfortunately most of them were city-bred Cockneys who had never wielded an axe and had no idea how to go about cultivating the land. Not surprisingly, the Barr colonists encountered terrible hardships, and only a few of the hardiest ones lasted as farmers. Yet even the bad publicity surrounding the adventure did not deter the continued growth of British settlement in the West.

Canada became the "land of the second chance" for many impoverished and underprivileged classes of people in Great Britain. Orphans and destitute persons, those often referred to as the "outcasts of London," had their fares to the Dominion paid by private charitable agencies such as the Salvation Army and the East End Emigration Fund. Another institution, Dr. Bernardo's Homes, sent more than twenty thousand British children to Canada between 1867 and 1914. These deserted or orphaned children were either placed with Canadian families, mostly in Ontario and Quebec, or cared for in rural training institutions.

The Autonomy Bills

Immigrants from Britain and the United States continued to be joined by a steady stream from continental Europe. To many inhabitants of the older sections of Canada, this was a cause for concern. English-Canadian imperialists worried about keeping "British stock dominant" in order to preserve Canada's allegiance to the Empire. French Canadians felt that the increasingly multi-ethnic composition of the West threatened their claim to full recognition for French-language rights. Leading voices in Quebec, such as Henri Bourassa and Conservative spokesman F.D. Monk, feared for the future of French Canadians in a Canada where they were becoming a declining minority and in a West where their numbers lagged behind several other groups. The small, scattered population of French Canadians in the West, unassisted by any substantial immigration from France or Quebec, seemed on the verge of being swamped by the flood of newcomers.

The anxieties of French Canadians uneasy about the cultural makeup of the population of the prairies came to a head in the debate over the political future of the North-West Territories. The dispute over provincial status for the area provoked a political crisis and provided much ammunition for Laurier's critics in both French and English Canada. The prime minister opened the public debate on a high note, pledging his faith in the promise of "Canada's century," but the whole affair soon degenerated into a wrangle over separate schools and the cultural rights of French-Canadian minorities.

Since 1901 the people of the Northwest had been demanding an end to their subordinate territorial status. Frederick Haultain, premier in the legislature of the North-West Territories, was pressuring Ottawa for the creation of a single province out of the vast prairie area. Eventually Laurier and his government responded to Haultain's arguments for provincial recognition. But instead of creating one new province, the Laurier government established two, each roughly as big as Ontario was at the time. At the urging of Clifford Sifton, the Dominion retained control of public lands for immigration purposes. A major controversy erupted, however, over what educational rights should be granted

By creating two provinces instead of one, Laurier sealed Haultain's political fate. The new provincial boundary separated Haultain from most of his Conservative followers, and both new provinces were launched with strong Liberal governments.

to the Catholic minorities in the new provinces of Saskatchewan and Alberta.

A compromise was eventually reached, and the Autonomy Bills of 1905 made Alberta and Saskatchewan full-fledged provinces. Yet the price was high for Sir Wilfrid Laurier. Clifford Sifton resigned from the cabinet over Laurier's original plan to allow Catholic (and other) minorities to establish their own tax-supported schools. In the end, the prime minister settled for a set of modest terms providing for the protection of minority rights. But this remarkable about-face did not win him back the support of Sifton, the strongest man the West had ever sent to Ottawa, and it also set Bourassa and other French-Canadian nationalists irrevocably against him.

The Assimilation Problem

The tens of thousands of newcomers lured to western Canada by the Dominion government came from more than thirty-five different countries speaking a babel of languages and practising over a hundred different religions. The question soon arose of what kind of society would emerge from such a conglomeration.

In a Canada which saw itself as the "brightest gem in the Crown of the British Empire," most native-born citizens took it for granted that their basically British ways were superior and would prevail. Immigrants would rush to be Canadianized. Yet for a long time the only real social agency active in most parts of the West was the North-West Mounted Police. While NWMP detachments worked hard and successfully to provide rough-and-

Saskatchewan's Inauguration Day ceremonies, September 4, 1905. Seated fourth from the left is Canada's Governor General, Earl Grey, now best remembered for presenting the country with the Grey Cup.

ready assistance for new immigrants, their influence could only be limited. Assimilation of the Ukrainians, Russians, Poles and other groups was left to some mysterious process of absorption, despite the fact that the newcomers were often hived away in ethnic bloc settlements, sometimes totally out of contact with other minorities or the English-speaking majority.

Few at the time doubted that complete assimilation of the "foreigners" was the desired goal, but not everyone expected it to happen automatically. As superintendent of All Peoples' Mission in the North End of Winnipeg, the young Methodist minister, J.S. Woodsworth, worked among immigrants and became intensely interested in the issue. "Within the past decade, a nation has been born," he wrote in a 1909 report. "English and Russians, French and Germans, Austrians and Italians, Japanese and Hindus—a mixed multitude, they are being dumped into Canada by a kind of endless chain. They sort themselves out after a fashion, and each seeks to find a corner somewhere. But how shall we weld this heterogeneous mass into one people? That is our problem."

In the opinion of many, including Clifford Sifton and other prominent figures such as John W. Dafoe, the Liberal editor of the Manitoba *Free Press*, the solution lay in the public school system. This is why Sifton was so adamantly opposed to the idea of tax-supported minority schools. Adult immigrants might or might not learn to speak much English; they might retain their traditional clothes and their "foreign" ways. But the public schools would teach their children English and with it the customs and manners of native-born Canadians. The next generation would be Canadian.

J.S. Woodsworth's concern over the assimilation problem led him to write his classic study *Strangers Within Our Gates* in 1909.

Backlash—A Wave of Exclusionism

Not every Canadian felt that an open door immigration policy was in the country's best interests. Sifton's successor, Frank Oliver, was one who wanted tighter controls on immigration. When he became minister in 1905, he moved almost immediately to make the Immigration Act more restrictive by broadening his powers to reject and deport. This change did not satisfy all the government's critics. Prominent Tory and Orangeman T.S. Sproule continued to complain that Canada had become "the dumping ground for the refuse of every country in the world."

Further changes in the Immigration Act in 1910 and a tightening of administrative procedures made it possible for the department to exclude whole classes of immigrants, particularly Asians, and American blacks, who were considered "undesirable." By 1911 Oliver was able to assert with accuracy that his policy was "restrictive, exclusive and selective" in comparison with his predecessor's.

PIONEERING IN SASKATCHEWAN
THE STORY OF CHARLES BROWN

Charles Brown was born March 28, 1894, at Dufferin in the Parry Sound District of central Ontario. The oldest of three boys, he lost his mother at age six and was raised by his father. When he was seventeen, Charles decided to leave Ontario and make his fortune in the "Last Best West." Travelling west on a harvest excursion train with two school friends, he landed at Kipling, Saskatchewan, in 1911. His first few months in the West were spent threshing grain and helping a cousin with the harvest.

During these months, Charles learned of the Canadian government's offer of one quarter-section of free land to anyone who would settle and farm in the West. He decided to stay. Since the land was being taken up quickly, Charles surveyed the area and chose a west half section (Section 20) in the White Valley District, about twenty-five kilometres southwest of Shaunavon.

Charles Brown spent his first year as a homesteader living in a sod shanty and working on a nearby ranch in order to scrape up enough money to buy a team of mares in foal. A younger brother, Jack, came west in the summer of 1912 to see Charles's land and decided to stay a while. Together the two Brown brothers obtained a contract to build 21 miles of fence for the T. Down Ranch. Out on the range Charles and Jack used a team and wagon and slept in a tent.

One of the most frightening experiences in Charles Brown's life occurred during the winter of 1912-13. Jack was away, and Charles was living alone in the sod shanty when a severe blizzard blew up. He was working in the barn and had just noticed the howling winds when he heard a loud noise coming from the direction of the hut. Looking out the barn door Charles saw the stove pipe fly right off the roof. He dashed back to the hut, but the fire had gone out and repeated attempts to light it failed. Finally giving up, he became aware of a regular clattering sound outside. The barn door! In his haste he had failed to latch it and it was swinging in the wind. Charles rushed to the hut door—it would not budge. In just a few minutes the wind had blown up such a drift that he was trapped in his sod hut. For three days the winds and snow blew, forcing Charles to remain in his unheatable hut. Throughout this ordeal he stayed in bed with his clothes on, periodically rubbing his feet to warm them up.

When the storm finally subsided, Charles rushed out to the barn to see how the horses had survived the wintry blast. The snow had drifted into the barn, burying the animals up to

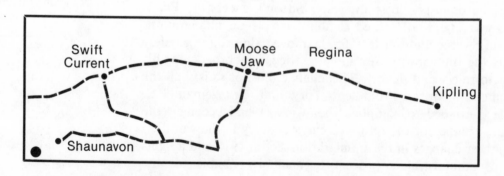

● *White Valley District*

their sides, but to his surprise they were stiff, but still alive. Charles decided then and there to build himself a proper wooden house as soon as spring arrived.

His closest neighbour was Ernest Stratton, who homesteaded the other half of Section 20. He was a native of northern Michigan, who had come to Saskatchewan after several years of driving mule-teams for American railway construction crews. Ernest was commonly seen driving four mules on an earth scraper, and always carried a whip when he drove any team of animals. But he was really a mild mannered and good natured man, and no one ever saw him strike an animal with his whip.

Determined to settle down, Ernest gradually built a five-room wooden house and a large barn on his homestead and, in 1916, decided to find a wife. With the help of a neighbour he placed an advertisement in a Detroit newspaper for "a housekeeper with agreement for marriage." The advertisement was answered by Mrs. Emily Webster, a widow with two children. Delighted with the success of his advertisement, Ernest sent the train fare for Emily and her two teenaged children, Ida and Harvey, to come west. As arranged, Emily and Ernest were married later that year.

The Brown and Stratton families became more than just neighbours in the years following Ernest's marriage to Emily Webster. A romance bloomed between neighbour Charles and Emily's daughter Ida. Three years after the Stratton marriage, nineteen-year-old Ida became Mrs. Charles Brown.

Adapted from Quarter Stake Echoes, *published by the South Shaunavon History Club, Shaunavon, Saskatchewan, 1981. Reprinted by permission of Ralph Brown.*

Sod hut

Charles Brown

Ralph Brown, one of Charles and Ida's eight children, with Grampa Stratton.

Emily and Ernest Stratton

Restricted Chinese Immigration
As early as 1885, the Canadian government had begun to restrict Chinese immigration by imposing a "head tax" of $50 that every Chinese person entering the country had to pay. Since some Chinese were still trickling in, the head tax was doubled in 1900 by the Laurier government. By 1903, it was $500, a staggering amount for a poor Chinese immigrant. At the same time, restrictive work legislation was passed in British Columbia, Saskatchewan, Ontario and Quebec.

Completely at odds with Oliver and the immigration restrictionists was the official spokesman for the Canadian Pacific Railway. As the major employer of immigrant labour, Sir William Van Horne favoured the retention of an open door policy. "Let them all come in," he said in 1906. "There is work for all. Every two or three men who come into Canada and do a day's work create new work for someone else to do. They are like a new dollar. Hand it out from the bank and it turns itself in value a dozen or more times a year."

The leaders of Canada's emerging labour movement, however, saw no sign of that profit ending up in a worker's pocket. The flood of immigrants looking for jobs seemed to be undercutting the campaigns of trade unions for better wages and working conditions. An underlying racial animosity compounded the problem. As one enraged delegate told the 1906 Trade and Labour Congress convention in Victoria, British Columbia: "In our years of [difficulties] we got on without the coolies, Chinese, Hindoos, Japanese and the riff-raff of Europe. Much more should we be able to do so now, without saddling prosperity with a coloured racial problem."

Keeping British Columbia White

Asian immigration was not part of the Laurier government's plan for western settlement. Chinese, Japanese and East Indian immigrants were regarded by the Interior Department and most Canadians as difficult to absorb, and therefore "undesirable." The centre of controversy over Oriental immigration was British Columbia. It was here that the vast majority of Asians entered Canada, and in the years from 1900 to 1908 record numbers of them arrived, the annual intake swelling from several hundred to roughly 12 000. Such dramatic increases stirred fears of the "yellow peril" that bigots had been warning British Columbians of for years.

Cries of "Keep British Columbia White" rang out and the demand for exclusion reached new heights. The year 1907 was a time of high unemployment and economic recession on the west coast, and increased immigration from the Far East was resented even more than it had been. Confronted with growing demands to bar the door to Asians, the Laurier government tightened up its immigration regulations. A heavier head tax was levied on Chinese immigrants, and a series of Orders-in-Council were issued to limit the entry of East Indians. Japan's status at that time as an ally of Britain and Canada's desire for access to Japanese markets necessitated more generous treatment, and a "Gentleman's Agreement" was negotiated with the Japanese government to voluntarily restrict the number of its citizens entering Canada.

The ugly face of anti-Orientalism showed itself in Vancouver

in the autumn of 1907. A federal-provincial dispute between Premier Richard McBride of British Columbia and the Laurier government over Asian exclusion legislation flared up. Soon an Asiatic Exclusion League was formed in Vancouver and plans were made for a parade through the Chinatown and Little Tokyo sections of the city. On the day of the march the protestors sang "Rule Britannia" and threw stones at Japanese store windows. A full-scale riot broke out. In the rioting, a band of Japanese immigrants turned on their attackers and gave them, in Sir Wilfrid Laurier's words, "a proper licking." A commission of inquiry headed by the deputy minister of labour, W.L. Mackenzie King, awarded compensation to the Japanese shopkeepers, but the real damage had been done; the riot of 1907 was remembered in British Columbia for many years.

Scene of the 1907 anti-Asian riot in Vancouver.

An Emerging Multi-ethnic Society

The social and cultural problems of the West and the harsh treatment meted out to many immigrants failed to slow the rapid development of the prairies. Census and production figures for 1911 told the tale. Farm settlement in Manitoba, Saskatchewan and Alberta had jumped from six million hectares in 1901 to twenty-three million at the end of the decade. Actual crop cultivation on western prairie lands had shown an amazing increase from just over a million to more than seven million hectares over the same ten years.

Despite Sifton's goal of channelling immigrants to agricultural lands, substantial numbers of newcomers either remained in the cities or ended up there after abandoning their homesteads. Winnipeg, western Canada's lone city in 1901, had grown into a small metropolis of 136 000 people by 1911. It was joined by major new urban centres, such as Calgary, Regina, Edmonton and Saskatoon, and hundreds of smaller towns.

Towns and cities were important in the West. Unlike eastern farmers who could produce most of their own food, prairie farmers grew grain to sell, not food to eat. They used the cash from their grain sales to buy food and clothing, implements and seed. They did their buying in the towns and the towns sprang up to supply the farmers' needs. After so many years of waiting, after the painfully slow growth of the 1880s and 1890s, the prairie West had been opened up.

The 1911 census, which showed the great growth of the West, also revealed the changing ethnic composition of the country. British and American immigrants had made up a majority of the newcomers, but the ratio of people of British origin in the total population had fallen from 60 to 55 percent. All cities in Canada now had their Jewish or Italian quarters, or their Chinatowns, but it was in the West that the variety was most evident. Over 40 percent of the population of Alberta and Saskatchewan was classified as "foreign." The West had taken on a polyglot pattern of ethnic settlements and was dotted with hundreds of towns boasting strange-sounding names like Veregin, Esterhazy, Bruderheim and Gimli. They were mixed in with towns whose names revealed the presence on the prairies of French and English cultures too: Dauphin and Lacombe and Prudhomme, Wolsely and Holdfast and Kipling. A Canadian mosaic was starting to form in the prairie West. You can see it today in the names on a map.

A new kind of Canadian society was being created on the prairies. Out of its hardship and successes, the diversity of its ethnic communities, the West developed a sense of its own identity. It was Canadian, but with a distinctive flavour. For most settlers, it was a place where everyone had a second chance. In the words of an English visitor, J.B. Bickersteth, the Canadian West was a kind of "Land of Open Doors," where hard work, competitive instincts and luck brought individual success and independence.

REVIEW AND DISCUSSION

Key People and Ideas
Explain the importance of each of the following as they are discussed in the chapter.

Clifford Sifton	"The Last Best West"
Cora Hind	"Men in sheepskin coats"
Georgina Binnie-Clarke	North Atlantic Trading Company
Frederick Haultain	"Land of the second chance"
J.S. Woodsworth	Autonomy Bills of 1905
John W. Dafoe	Asiatic Exclusion League
Frank Oliver	

Analysing the Issues
Answer each of the following questions, which deal with important issues raised in the chapter.

1. What methods did Clifford Sifton use to encourage immigration to the Canadian West?
2. What conditions were faced by the new settlers in the West? What particular problems confronted women who settled in the West?
3. What political problems did Laurier face when he established the provinces of Saskatchewan and Alberta?
4. What was the nature of the concern and opposition towards the open immigration policies of Clifford Sifton?

Questions and Discussion

Think carefully about each of the following questions and discuss the issues they raise.

1. The advertising which was used to promote immigration to the Canadian West presented a rosy picture which was in contrast to what many immigrants found when they arrived in Canada. Did the Canadian government mislead potential immigrants or did the long-term advantages of life in Canada outweigh the hardships they faced at first? Justify your opinion.
2. Immigration policy has always been an area of controversy in Canada. When Canadian governments have instituted "open door" immigration policies, as Clifford Sifton did around the turn of the century, Canadians have expressed strong feelings both in support of the policy and in opposition. Is an "open door" policy good for Canada or do you think the government should impose tight restrictions on immigration? Justify your opinion.

4

PATTERNS OF GROWTH

Canada entered the twentieth century enjoying the benefits of a buoyant economy. The industrialized cities of Europe had opened up expanding markets for Canadian grain, and the arrival of many thousands of new immigrants in western Canada made it possible for the country to meet that demand. But the booming growth and new dynamism was not confined to the agricultural West. New forces were unleashed in central Canada, the Maritimes and the frontier hinterlands as a return of business confidence brought British and American investment capital pouring into the country.

In July 1903, Sir Wilfrid Laurier made a stirring speech that caught the mood and promise of the age: "The flood tide is upon us that leads to fortune; if we let it pass it may never recur again. If we let it pass, the voyage of our national life, bright as it is today, will be arrested in the shallows. We cannot wait because time will not wait."

The settlement of the prairies set off a "Wheat Boom" and placed Canada on the threshold of national economic expansion. Conditions were ripe for industrial growth. The booming agricultural economy of the West created a new set of demands: thousands of newcomers had to be clothed and sheltered; new banks had to be opened to provide capital and rail lines built to carry the produce to market. Canada's growing cities, too, held out the promise of expansion, providing labour for factories and consumers demanding an increasing array of goods.

The "Golden Age" of Prosperity

Through the fifteen years of Liberal rule, Canada experienced a time of unparalleled prosperity. There were ups and downs in the economy—even a mild recession in 1907-08—but over the years population and industrial production grew at a faster rate than ever before. Towns in the West, such as Winnipeg, Calgary and Vancouver, mushroomed into cities. In central Canada the cities of Montreal and Toronto swelled with new immigrants and blossomed into metropolises. The country's output of manufactured goods increased in value from $215 million in 1900 to $564 million in 1910. Factories hummed, people had jobs, and there were markets for Canadian goods. It seemed like a Golden Age for most Canadians, and for Laurier's Liberal party.

Expectations of continued growth were high, and often inflated. "Expansion equals progress" was the popular attitude of the time. Surveying the national wealth in 1903, Joseph W. Flavelle, the wealthy Toronto pork-packer, boasted with some exaggeration: "These drops are but the promise of the shower that is to come." Few recognized that when this growth came prosperity would be distributed unevenly, favouring some regions or classes over others.

Opposite page:
Telephone repair tower, c. 1902. Although the first telephone exchange in Canada went into operation in 1878, it was during the Laurier years that telephones in private homes really proliferated. The number of telephones in the country jumped from 63 000 in 1901 to 354 000 ten years later.

A New Venture in Railway Building

"In these days of wonderful development," Laurier boldly proclaimed in 1903, it is "our duty, immediate and imperative," to build a second transcontinental railway. With these words he announced the beginning of Canada's last and longest phase of railway building. This decision also initiated a bold new financing venture, fraught with risks and difficulties.

The time seemed right for a new Canadian transcontinental railway. As immigrants poured into Canada, as wheat production in the West soared and business expanded everywhere, the Canadian Pacific Railway was unable to meet all the demands placed upon it. The CPR had been built in the 1880s to serve the needs of the 1890s. By 1901 the quantities of wheat being hauled out of the West had become so great that the CPR could not handle the business. The Winnipeg terminals became jammed with grain each year. Western farmers grew increasingly unhappy with the CPR's monopoly of the transportation that was essential to them. Many even resorted to shipping out their grain on American railways.

Laurier's announcement that the government was willing to support a new railway building program came as no great surprise. He had, in fact, begun negotiating in 1902 with Charles M. Hays of the Grand Trunk Railway Company and with William Mackenzie and Donald Mann of the Canadian Northern Railway. The Grand Trunk was the most important rail system in eastern Canada, while the Canadian Northern ran many short lines in the West. Both groups had plans to extend their lines from coast to coast.

Mackenzie and Mann, two Ontario-born promoters, were the most colourful figures in the new age of railway building. After some early experience working for the CPR, the two men had formed a partnership, secured financial aid from the Manitoba government, and built a small 160-kilometre line northwest of Winnipeg. They used promotional stunts to compete with the CPR and win the loyalty of Manitoba farmers. On one occasion, large quantities of seed grain were purchased and given away free to settlers on the line; their trains were reported to stop often to deliver a hind of beef or an invitation to supper for a single farm family.

The gimmickry worked. With the generous help of the Manitoba government, Mackenzie and Mann leased 500 kilometres of Canadian lines built earlier by a now bankrupt American company and consolidated their holdings to form the Canadian Northern Company. In five short years Mackenzie and Mann had become heroes on the prairies.

Laurier was uneasy about Mackenzie and Mann's overnight success and was inclined to favour the Grand Trunk's scheme. But common sense really seemed to suggest that the two compa-

Slim and intense, William Mackenzie was the financial wizard of the partnership, tapping Canadian governments for a total of $250 million for their railway projects. The cocky, tough, barrel-chested Mann played the role of railway builder, responsible for keeping construction moving at a break-neck pace.

nies should combine their efforts to build a second transcontinental line from Quebec City to the Pacific. The Grand Trunk and the Canadian Northern were rivals, however, and refused to pool their resources in spite of Laurier's persuasive efforts. Finally Laurier gave in. Ignoring the strong objections of both Clifford Sifton and A.G. Blair, the Minister of Railways, he pushed through measures which provided both companies with government financing and support for their schemes.

To Blair, the building of two new competitive transcontinental railways seemed indefensible on economic grounds. The Minister of Railways attacked the plan as a "senseless railway transaction" and resigned from the cabinet in protest.

A $200 Million Vote-Catcher
Laurier's grandiose railway policies may not have made economic sense, but they proved to be a political bonanza. In the West, farmers wanted as much competition as possible for the unpopular CPR. The plan was applauded as well in Ontario, where industries would be busy supplying nails, construction equipment and rolling stock for the new lines. In Quebec, French-Canadian *nationalistes* and the Quebec Catholic church saw the new railways as an aid to their schemes for northern colonization, which were already underway. Even the Maritimes, long neglected by federal governments, stood to benefit from a new rail line to Moncton and the jobs it would bring. It was, as the opposition Tories charged, a "$200 million vote catcher . . . designed to carry elections rather than passengers."

Officials of the Canadian Northern did their utmost to win the good will of prairie farmers. "Service was our motto," one later remarked. "We had more stopping places to the ten miles I think than any railway in the world. Only a few of them were on the timetable."

The Railway Building Boom

Once the go-ahead was given for the two new transcontinentals, the Grand Trunk Pacific, the Canadian Northern and the CPR quickly became engaged in cut-throat competition. Between 1903 and 1915 Mackenzie and Mann built a railroad of over sixteen thousand kilometres, created more than a hundred prairie towns and established a financial empire floating on government bonds. Charles M. Hays and the Grand Trunk Pacific were not to be out-done. In the struggle to keep pace with its rivals, the GTP spent $50 million for "the finest road on the prairies," put up 131 grain elevators, "grid-ironed" Saskatchewan and crossed eighty high-ways in Alberta without waiting for government permission. The CPR retaliated with an expansion of its own. Feeder lines in On-tario and the prairies were upgraded; some two thousand men were put to work cutting grades and digging tunnels in Kicking Horse Pass; and the company's steamship operations were ex-tended to the Atlantic shipping trade.

The pace of construction was feverish and money was spent recklessly. Under the terms of its agreement with the GTP, the government lavished almost a quarter of a billion dollars on the construction of a line crossing the Canadian Shield from Quebec to Winnipeg, hundreds of kilometres north of the CPR line, and erected the famous Quebec Bridge, the world's longest cantilever span, which twice collapsed, killing seventy-five men. In the issu-ing of contracts, corruption was rampant. Scores of Liberal hangers-on bought up and inflated the prices of land along the right-of-way. Contracts were padded and building the new line across northern Quebec and Ontario cost twice as much and took twice as long as projected. Laurier's biographer, O.D. Skelton, called it "the most corrupting single factor since Confederation."

In the first decade of the new century, railway building was a catalyst for industrialization. One in three wage earners in eastern Canada worked for a railway or a company manufacturing rail-way supplies. Some sixty to eighty thousand men each year found work clearing and grading the land, laying ties and tracks. Rail-way companies consumed gigantic quantities of timber, steel, dynamite, tools and bridge-building materials. Orders poured into the steel companies for rails. New locomotives and freight cars were built. Hundreds of new grain elevators, lake freighters and warehouses were constructed. Every little town had its railway depot, and in cities like Montreal, Toronto and Winnipeg, huge new stations were erected to handle the growing number of rail passengers. Many of Canada's famous "Grand Hotels" such as the Château Laurier in Ottawa, the Fort Garry in Winnipeg and the Empress in Victoria were constructed in this period, offering luxury living for travellers.

Life on the Line

Railway construction workers did not share many of the benefits of the boom. Laurier's immigration policy supplied the railways with thousands of unskilled central and southern European workers. Railway contractors and "bosses" on the line considered them to be "cheap, obedient and industrious," and therefore ideal for the hazardous work on the grade. Workers—popularly known as "blanketstiffs"—jumped from job to job packing their few belongings in their blanket rolls and, during the slow seasons, sawed trees in British Columbia and harvested wheat on the prairies.

Life in the railway bunkhouse camps was very rough. "The whole surroundings," Edmund Bradwin, who taught English and reading and writing to the men in the camps, later recalled, "were fitter far for the stabling of cattle than the abode of men" and "at a whiff therefrom a well reared pig would grunt disapproval." In their travels from job to job, itinerant workers tramped along the tracks they had laid or rode in boxcars. Life was often reduced to a job, a spree, another job, another spree.

The Boom Goes Sour

The new railways were in serious trouble almost from the start. Rapidly rising production costs and financial misadventures had combined to put the railway companies heavily into debt. Even before the new continental lines were fully in use, the outbreak of the First World War in 1914 cut the stream of settlers travelling to the West. British and foreign investment in railway projects dried up. With three transcontinental lines, Canada had more kilometres of railway than it needed. This led to ruinous competition for whatever business was available, leaving the new companies on the verge of bankruptcy.

The financial burden of Laurier's costly railway schemes passed on to his successor, Robert L. Borden. Borden's Conservative government had no choice but to bail the companies out of their difficulties. Millions of dollars of taxpayers' money and the country's reputation were at stake. Temporary assistance was granted, and eventually in 1923 the Canadian government took over the Grand Trunk Pacific and Canadian Northern lines and merged them into the system known as the Canadian National Railways.

Metals, Timber and Men

The railway boom was matched by a tremendous expansion in the exploitation of the Dominion's mineral and forest resources. The forests and rock of the Canadian Shield and the British Columbia hinterland, long the preserve of the fur trade, now came under the probing pick of the prospector and the heavy axe of the logger.

The "Blanket Stiff"

He built the ROAD—
With others of his CLASS,
    he built the road,
Now o'er it, many a weary mile,
    he packs his load,
Chasing a JOB. Spurred on
    by HUNGERS goad
He walks and walks,
    and wonders why
In H--L, he built the road.

This development of natural resources brought prosperity to many parts of the Dominion and sustained the pace of Canada's industrial expansion.

The Klondike Gold Rush

In the summer of 1896 George Carmack and two Indian friends, Skookum Jim and Tagish Charlie, spied several shiny nuggets in the Bonanza Creek, a tributary of the Klondike River. They had been looking for gold and now they had found it. They drove stakes into the ground to mark their find and hurried back to register their claim with the local Mounted Police detachment.

As word of the discovery spread, the lure of gold sent prospectors crazy with excitement. Tens of thousands of fortune seekers from the Dominion, from California and from all over the world converged on Dawson, at the junction of the Yukon and Klondike rivers. Within three years of the first discovery, all the creeks around the Klondike had been staked out by gold-diggers.

There were several ways to get to the Yukon gold fields, but many of the gold seekers scrambled to them over the treacherous route known as the "Trail of '98." After travelling by boat to the port of Skagway, the hordes of prospectors climbed the steep slopes through the Chilkoot Pass in the Coastal Range to the headwaters of the Yukon River. They carried all their supplies on their backs, since the slopes were too steep for pack animals. After crossing the Pass, they built rafts and floated almost a thousand kilometres down the Yukon River to Dawson. Despite hardships and danger, during the winter of 1897-98 alone an estimated 22 000 men and women made the trip through the Chilkoot Pass, in search of instant riches.

The Klondike Gold Rush spawned a host of tales and legends. The sudden riches, the heroic feats, the shady characters, the tragedies and rowdiness of the mining frontier were immortalized in poems and songs such as "The Trail of '98," "The Spell of the Yukon," and "Dangerous Dan McGrew." Men like "Big Alex" McDonald, who bought a claim on the Eldorado Creek for a sack of flour, made twenty million dollars, squandered it all and died penniless in a log cabin, became part of Canadian folklore. And stories of Dawson as a rip-roaring gold town of saloons and music halls live on in popular memory.

For all its romance and reputed rowdiness, the Klondike town of Dawson was very different from the entry port of Skagway in the Alaska Panhandle. Both were classic boom towns which had swelled almost overnight from huddles of shacks to lively cities. However, while Skagway was a wild, lawless town ruled by "Soapy" Smith and a gang of outlaws, Dawson was remarkably orderly for a frontier settlement. Acts of rowdiness and drunkenness were common, but no one was allowed to carry fire-

Kathleen Eloisa Rockwell, better known as "Klondike Kate," "Queen of the Yukon" and "Sweetheart of the Sourdoughs."

arms within the city limits, and the streets were often cleared by the local North-West Mounted Police. True to the Canadian tradition, order prevailed and NWMP justice reigned supreme.

Huge fortunes were made—and lost—in the Yukon gold rush. Between 1896 and 1904 gold seekers extracted $100 million worth of the metal from the ground. In 1898 the fantastic inflow of people had compelled the Dominion to make the Yukon a territory with its own government, sending the district leaping ahead of the rest of Canada's North. But by 1904 the boom had ended, leaving the Yukon government to manage near-deserted towns and the remnants of a gold rush.

Less spectacular but no less important mining developments were also taking place in southern British Columbia. Here extensive mining operations were started for reasons associated with American westward expansion. Mining promoters and businessmen from the neighbouring states of Montana and Washington had opened up operations to meet the growing industrial demands of the United States. By the late 1890s and early 1900s southern British Columbia had become a virtual northern "hinterland" for

Ant-like, one right behind the other, a seemingly endless line of gold-seekers climb the 1500 icy steps to the summit of the Chilkoot pass. Martha Black later wrote of the experience: "We clung to the stunted pines, spruce roots, jutting rocks. In some places the path was so narrow that, to move at all, we had to use our feet tandem-fashion. Above only the granite walls. Below death leering at us."

Sam Steele, commanding officer of the North-West Mounted Police. Steele became known as the "Lion of the Yukon" as a result of his firmness in establishing law and order amond the hordes of adventurers swarming into the Klondike.

the American mining industry. The Kootenay district was dotted with silver, lead and zinc mines; copper was being mined at Sullivan and gold near Rossland. At Trail a giant, belching smelter was erected to refine the loads of ore from neighbouring mines. It was not until the CPR built a line through the district, however, that British and Canadian investors began to pour capital into the British Columbia mining ventures.

Developing the "New Ontario"

Just when the Klondike rush was petering out, a sensational silver find in northern Ontario set off a new mining boom. According to popular legend, Alfred LaRose, a blacksmith working on the Temiskaming and Northern Ontario Railway in 1903, threw his hammer at something he thought was the eyes of a fox shining in the glow from his campfire. The next morning to his amazement he discovered that his hammer had struck a silver vein. What luck! It was the world's largest silver deposit. News spread like wildfire. Suddenly the town of Cobalt became the centre of a flourishing mining district.

The Cobalt mining boom, however, was no accident of nature. Through its public investment in railways, the Ontario government had created favourable conditions for the exploitation of northern resources by Toronto capital and enterprise. The Temiskaming and Northern Ontario Railway, built with generous provincial subsidies and running right through the centre of the Cobalt camps, made the district easily accessible, linking it to Toronto through North Bay.

The thirty square kilometres of northern Ontario wilderness known as the Cobalt district was transformed completely by the silver strike. By the end of 1906, the Cobalt and Kerr Lakes area had been staked out in thousands of small, overlapping claims, and some 584 mining companies had been chartered to sell millions of dollars worth of shares to an eager public. Cobalt had grown on the marshy shore of Lake Temiskaming into a booming town of 7000 people. Life was so wild that, in one highly publicized incident, a man was killed by a dynamite blast set off by a silver-crazed prospector looking for treasure on the main street of the new town. The lake close to town came to be called "Poison Lake" after mining companies began dumping gray cyanide slime into its once clear waters. Trainloads of veteran and amateur prospectors, stock promoters and speculators flocked to Cobalt in the summer months—setting off stampedes to buy Cobalt silver stocks on Toronto's Bay Street and New York's Wall Street.

The dream of striking it rich remained just that, however—a dream—for all but a few Cobalt district mining companies. The silver veins of the area promised great riches, but many ignorant investors fell prey to fraudulent schemes. Some operations, like the wildcat companies at nearby Larder Lake, sold worthless shares to the public and funnelled money into the pockets of the promoters. Of all the companies formed during the Cobalt boom, only twenty-nine ventures developed producing mines, and half of these were American-owned. These mines, however, yielded $114 million worth of silver, making it the second most important mineral mined in Canada.

The silver strike at Cobalt spurred exploration throughout the Ontario northland, known popularly as the "New Ontario." Within a few years huge deposits of gold were uncovered at Timmins, Kirkland Lake and in the Porcupine district. Mining companies were formed by enterprising men like Noah Timmins and Sandy McIntyre, who put Timmins on the map as the "gold nugget" capital of Canada. No longer considered a wasteland of barren rock, swamps and blackflies, the Canadian Shield was beginning to realize its resource potential.

In northern Ontario the rapid growth of the mining industry was made possible by publicly financed railways and exploration and development money from Bay Street and New York. Control of profitable mines often ended up in New York, but as more and more of the Shield was opened up, Bay Street emerged as the centre of its financial activities. The mining areas of the Ontario northland rapidly became part of Toronto's expanding hinterland and area of influence. "It is upon the prospector and the miner," the Toronto Board of Trade claimed in 1906, "that the New Ontario must depend to increase in population and wealth."

The Assault on the Forest

Forestry lacked the glitter of the mining rushes. Yet Canada was endowed with one of the world's greatest natural stands of timber. This wealth of forest resources seemed inexhaustible, and when prosperity returned to the North American economy in the 1890s, the forest industry became caught up in the rapid pace of resource development.

The boom years saw a tremendous increase in the demand for Canadian timber. During the 1890s Canada's forests supplied the British and American markets with sawn lumber, and in the first decade of the new century, produced vast amounts of planks to meet new demands for building materials in Canada, the United States and other parts of the world. Most of the timber came from the white pine stands of Ontario, but British Columbia, too, experienced a run on its forests. Douglas fir, spruce and cedar made excellent lumber for growing western cities and towns, barns and grain elevators. A rising demand for newsprint in the United States was satisfied by aggressive Canadian and foreign investors who established giant pulp and paper mills in Ontario, Quebec and New Brunswick.

THE LIFE OF A SILVER MINER

The discovery of rich silver nuggets in 1903 at Cobalt Lake, 160 kilometres north of North Bay, near the Ontario–Quebec border, touched off a spectacular mining boom. Prospectors, writers, stock promoters, mining engineers and politicians from every corner of the world rushed to Cobalt to seek their fortune. The silver rush brought an outpouring of optimism. "Here," boasted the Cobalt *Nugget* in 1909, "the ground breeds millionaires. One bumps into them everywhere."

The Cobalt mining district developed as a poor man's lode camp. "Fortune seekers" and seasoned prospectors scurried over the barren, rocky and thin forest staking their claims. Because the ore was so rich and close to the surface, little capital was required to begin production. Miners tore great vertical slashes in the face of the cliffs and gouged huge "glory holes" in the ground. Early shipments, dug out by hand using pick and shovel, secured enough profit to enable some owners to purchase machinery, erect headframes and sink mine shafts. At the height of the boom, the Cobalt camp had twenty-nine shipping mines.

A Miners' Week

The first prospectors at Cobalt were high-spirited adventurers who often arrived with little more than a small grubstake and a prayer. Conditions were so overcrowded in the Cobalt boarding houses that many miners could only rent a bed in town on an eight-hour shift basis. Others found lodgings in company-owned bunkhouses charging sixty cents a day for room and board.

Saturday evenings were the highlight of any week. Hordes of workers poured into Cobalt where movies, dance halls, penny arcades, pool rooms, shooting galleries and "blind pigs" catered to the tastes of fun-loving miners.

Yet visitors and longtime residents alike all remarked on the lack of violence and disorder in Cobalt. The Ontario Mines Act prohibited the sale of intoxicating liquor within five miles (8 km) of a producing mine and the strongest drink available in the saloons of Cobalt was O'Keefe's Star Beer, a hops and malt concoction containing less than 2 percent alcohol. Nevertheless, many miners travelled regularly to four licensed hotels in the nearby town of Haileybury, others brewed their own "hooch" known as "Cobalt Bloom," and some patronized a host of local bootleggers.

Working Underground

The life of the Cobalt hardrock miner was difficult. Safety measures in the early years were almost nonexistent. The blasters had to defrost the dynamite in warm water, or by sticking it in their pockets. Holes were usually hand drilled. Where pneumatic drills were used, they created thick clouds of dust and were tabbed "widow makers." The muck was extracted by shovel. In the first years mine labourers crept around in dark catacombs lit only by candlelight, often gasping for breath in shafts deficient in oxygen. By the end of 1912 the mines of Cobalt had claimed over a hundred lives, yet the Ontario Bureau of Mines openly boasted that only "an average of one man" was killed per $170 000 of ore production.

Early prospector

Wage Schedule at Standard Cobalt Mines per 9-Hour Shift, July 1908

Machine Men	$3.50
Machine Helpers	$3.00
Hand Miners	$3.00
Pumpmen	$3.00
Timbermen	$3.50
Timber Helpers	$2.75
Trammers	$2.75
Muckers	$2.75
Cage Tenders	$3.00
Hoistmen	$3.10
Deckmen	$2.50
Head Blacksmith	$4.00
Blacksmith	$3.50
Surface Labour	$2.50

Cobalt, c. 1910

A veteran miner's face showed the hard life he had led.

Ready to go down the shaft.

In 1904, lumbermen like these would have been paid $25 to $30 a month with bed and board.

Profits were the driving force behind the relentless assault on the Canadian forest. Once the white pine stocks in Michigan, Wisconsin and Minnesota were exhausted, American lumbermen moved northward, mainly into the forests of New Ontario. In defence of the Canadian industry, Ontario lumbermen convinced the provincial government to impose a "manufacturing condition" on sawlog exporters, prohibiting the export of raw, unprocessed logs to the United States. But the restriction had little effect on the rate of cutting. American firms simply moved across the border, mills and all, and continued to haul bargeloads of wood products back to the United States. Forests were chopped out recklessly in an onslaught of wanton destruction. Conservation measures eventually came, but too late to save the last great stands of white pine in North America.

The Age of Enterprise
In the boom years of the Laurier era Canada's business leaders were depicted in the popular press as national benefactors. Rapid economic growth fed the popular mythology. Businessmen, it was said, were the "nation-building class"—driving steel rails through the wilderness, erecting busy factories, blasting metals out of the Shield, unlocking the power of Niagara.

Yet industrial expansion in the Laurier years was not all the work of Canadian businessmen—nor were their motives necessarily of the highest. The protective tariff, first adopted by Sir John

A. Macdonald in 1879 and sustained by the Laurier government, sheltered native industries from the full force of American and other foreign competition. Railway-building was heavily subsidized; natural resources were exploited freely; labour unions were weak; taxes were low and profit-making was almost completely unrestrained. To some critics, this business expansion amounted to a "Great Barbeque," or businessman's paradise.

As the Dominion entered the new century, electricity replaced steam as the driving force in industry and gave birth to a new generation of electrically driven factory machines. These advances boosted productivity and production and brought far-reaching changes in the scale and organization of industrial enterprises. Between the early 1890s and 1911 large corporations all but supplanted small-scale, owner-operated enterprises as the dominant form of business. A great wave of business mergers and consolidations, which reached a crest between 1909 and 1912, gave birth to such giant companies as Dominion Steel, CCM, Canada Bread, Dominion Canners and Canada Cement.

Confronted with this massive merger wave, the Laurier government took a *laissez-faire* stance. It also welcomed the spill-over of huge American enterprises into Canada. The protective tariff which sheltered Canadian industries did not make any distinction on grounds of ownership. Foreign-owned companies producing goods in Canada enjoyed the same advantage as Canadian-owned ones. This encouraged many American companies to jump the tariff wall by establishing branch plants in Canada. So did iron and steel export bounties, the "made-in-Canada" provisions of Dominion railway legislation, and Canadian patent laws.

American companies moved into Canada in a big way. The number of American-owned branch factories in the country jumped from about 70 in 1900 to 215 in 1909 and 450 by 1914. U.S. Tobacco, United States Rubber, Coca-Cola, Westinghouse, Quaker Oats, Sherwin-Williams Paint, Gillette Safety Razor and General Motors, to name only a few, established Canadian subsidiaries during this period. The flood of American capital was welcomed by Canadian governments—federal, provincial and municipal—actively competing with one another for a share of industrial development. Native capitalists, including the leaders of the Canadian Manufacturers' Association, often seemed awe-struck by the marvels of "Yankee enterprise." "The more money that we can induce to come here," a leading business journal proclaimed in 1908, "the better for all of us."

During the heyday of industrial growth, Canadian businessmen developed their own unique pattern of thought. Most prominent business leaders, like Toronto's Timothy Eaton, Calgary cattle king Pat Burns and banker Sir Edmund Walker, professed to be apostles of free enterprise and *laissez-faire*. Prosperity, they

Industrial Mergers Between 1900 and 1908, the Monetary Times *reported 8 industrial mergers, involving 57 firms and $43 million in authorized capital. In 1909 and 1910 alone, 33 mergers were reported involving 272 firms and almost $300 million in capital.*

claimed, depended on business success, and business success, measured in profits, resulted from the pursuit by individuals of their own interests, free of any government regulation or interference.

The actions of Canadian businessmen often belied their words, however. Railway magnates such as Mackenzie and Mann, C.M. Hays and William Van Horne, relied heavily on support from governments to finance their lines. Businessmen, large and small, seeing themselves operating in a risky, highly competitive market, often urged the government to protect them through tariffs, export duties and early-closing laws. Even in the profitable boom years, the uncertainties of open competition were too much for many businessmen. Eventually, in many cases, they turned to the state for aid in their struggles to earn a "living profit." Some even went so far as to support government ownership of resources.

The Fight for Public Power

By the turn of the century Ontario's expanding factories and mining and pulpwood operations had created tremendous new demands for cheap sources of power. Coal shortages, caused by a 1902 coal strike in the United States, had sent fuel prices skyrocketing and intensified the search for new energy sources. "Hydro"—water-generated electric power—seemed to be the answer, and a host of private companies scrambled to gain the lucrative municipal franchises for its distribution.

During the decade spanning 1900, hydro power came into increasing use in Ontario's factories, homes and municipal facilities. Both business and civil leaders had begun to develop schemes for its economical delivery to industry and to the public. By 1896 electric power was being transmitted from Niagara Falls to Buffalo, New York. Within a few years Toronto businessmen, headed by William Mackenzie, Frederic Nicholls and financier Henry Pellatt, began to develop a plan to provide electrical power for Ontario's industry. Civic and business leaders in smaller western Ontario centres objected strongly. They feared that "Hogtown" would gain control of the riches of Niagara—and they sought a scheme that would ensure a fair distribution of electricity.

Hydro was considered such a valuable energy source that demands arose for public ownership. A popular movement, led by the dynamic and hard-driving Mayor of London, Adam Beck, and supported by Ontario manufacturers, local Boards of Trade and city councils, demanded government ownership lest the production, delivery and sale of electricity fall into the hands of privately owned, profit-seeking "monopolies." As a result, the Hydro-Electric Power Commission of Ontario was created in 1906 as a publicly owned utility. The idea of Ontario Hydro en-

joyed popular support, but it was also a triumph for business-men's "socialism"—a unique aspect of the Canadian Conservative tradition. Some other provinces followed Ontario's example and established government ownership of hydro-electricity.

Industrialization and the Maritimes

The economy of the Maritime provinces underwent a rapid transition during the Laurier years. As the region entered the new century, the main thrust of business initiative shifted away from its old reliance on fish and timber exports. The boom in central Canada made coal a resource with great development potential. As a result, Maritime entrepreneurs turned their attention to developing coal and other mineral resources closely related to the needs of central Canadian manufacturers.

The Maritimers' industrial initiatives worked. The region's iron and steel industry, based on the iron and coal resources of Cape Breton, flourished—then diversified into the manufacture of a wide range of steel products. By 1900 the main enterprise—Nova Scotia Steel and Coal Company—was thriving. A second major coal producer, Dominion Iron and Steel, soon branched out into full-scale steel production by opening its Sydney works.

This Sault Ste. Marie pulp mill was part of a giant industrial complex built in the 1890s by American entrepreneur Francis Hector Clergue. At its height, Clergue's Soo Industries included iron and steel mills, a pulp and paper company, shipping services and a company supplying water and light to the town. It seemed to be one of the great financial success stories of the era—until 1903 when the whole spectacular enterprise came tumbling down. Clergue had over-extended his credit and, unable to pay his debts, declared bankruptcy. The Ontario government rescued some of the businesses.

The progress of these two corporations was spectacular. By 1907 they were producing over one-half of Canada's pig iron and marketing their products nationwide. Aided by the protective tariff and the Intercolonial Railway's favourable freight rates, Maritime manufacturers won a large share of the expanding market for steel and other products in the Canadian West.

While Maritime industries expanded, however, control of the region's development was transferred largely to St. James St., Montreal's financial and stock market centre. Servicing the new Maritime industries had set off a wave of financial mergers. When this flurry of mergers ended, a host of Maritime banks had been swallowed up by financial giants with headquarters in Montreal. This loss of financial control led to a flight of capital from the Maritime provinces. Just as the region began to enjoy the benefits of industrialization, the central Canadian banks proceeded to divert the savings of Maritimers for investment outside the region.

French Canada and the New Industrial Order

While the Maritimes struggled for a share of industrialization, Quebec experienced a phase of economic change and growth. Since the mid-nineteenth century, the St. Lawrence Valley area of the province had been the home of an emerging manufacturing industry. This early industrial structure was based primarily on light manufacturing such as shoe, textile and clothing factories, and only secondarily on heavy manufacturing, like iron and steel and rail equipment operations. With the spread of factory and power-driven machine production after about 1850, most manufacturing was carried on in Montreal, Trois-Rivières, and other urban communities.

As Quebec entered the new century, the province's industrial base was transformed by a series of events connected with the return of North American economic prosperity. Settlement of the prairies, economic growth in the United States, and an inflow of American capital and technology stimulated business activity in Quebec as in other parts of Canada. The sewing machine, the phonograph and the bicycle became widely affordable consumer products. Technological advances, such as new pulp and paper processes and hydro-electric power generation methods created opportunities for profit-seeking entrepreneurs willing to invest in Quebec's forest and mineral resources. The result was a spurt of industrialization further expanding Quebec's manufacturing base.

By 1911 Quebec was no longer a predominantly rural society. Almost half its people lived in cities and towns. Only one-third of Quebec's population still worked in agriculture, and Quebec's economic growth matched that of Ontario. Many prominent French-speaking Quebeckers, and particularly Catholic Church leaders, saw the rapid pace of industrialization and the resulting

Opposite page: Winter Carnival construction, Quebec City, 1896.

urbanization as a development that posed dangers as well as opportunities. English-speaking capitalists moved strongly into Quebec's resource industries, establishing huge companies to export pulpwood, to harness hydro-electric power and to supply western settlers with manufactured goods. Some enterprising French Canadians, like Rodolphe Forget, J.D. Rolland and François Béique, became millionaires in the business bonanza of the Laurier years. But for the most part, French-Canadian businessmen were excluded from the emerging industrial elite.

This naturally caused resentment, but of even greater concern to many Quebec leaders was the mere fact of urbanization. They felt strongly that the survival of French Canadians as a people depended on the preservation of their traditional way of life. Now they saw the old Catholic rural values—attachment to the land, faith in the family and the Church—as threatened by those who put the pursuit of wealth above the worship of God, and material welfare ahead of spiritual peace.

In this atmosphere of social concern, a number of Quebec organizations emerged to fight for the survival of French-Canadian ways. The most influential of these *nationaliste* movements was *La Ligue Nationaliste Canadienne*, founded in 1903 by a group of ten young Quebec intellectuals. Its unofficial leader was Henri Bourassa, the idealistic and fiercely independent politician who had broken with Laurier over the issue of Canada'a participation in the Boer War. Their nationalism was, in large part, a reaction against the new industrialization dominated and directed by Anglo-Canadians. They campaigned to restore faith in the Church and its leadership and to reverse the migration of French Canadians to the cities by expanding the colonization of northern Quebec.

The colonization movement did succeed in opening up some farmland, settling communities and creating rudimentary services in such previously unsettled regions as the upper Ottawa River, the Gatineau, Saint-Maurice, Saguenay and Lac Saint-Jean areas. Unfortunately, a large proportion of the new territories was poor farmland, and the movement did little to increase agricultural activity or the average annual incomes of French-speaking Quebeckers.

In spite of the colonization movement and other attempts to preserve traditional French-Canadian ways, Quebec by the end of the Laurier years was fast becoming an urban and industrial society. The feared loss of identity, however, did not occur. In fact, when combined with the challenges posed by British imperialism and signs of hostility in other provinces, the new economic conditions, with *les Anglais* in control of most of the great industrial enterprises in the province, were making French Canadians feel even more like a distinct "national" community.

With the possible exception of Quebec, Canada by the late Laurier years semed to be a society brimming with optimism and national confidence. Outwardly all the signs seemed to suggest a future of glorious prosperity for the nation. The patterns of growth, however, differed greatly from region to region. The benefits of economic expansion had been distributed unevenly. Millions of Canadians neither shared fully in the prosperity nor in the sense of confidence in great achievements and rewards to come.

REVIEW AND DISCUSSION

Key People and Ideas
Explain the importance of each of the following as they are discussed in the chapter.

Joseph W. Flavelle "Trail of '98"
Charles M. Hays "Poison Lake"
William Mackenzie The "nation-building class"
Donald Mann Branch plants
George Carmack Hydro-Electric Power Commission
Alfred La Rose   of Ontario
Noah Timmins Nova Scotia Steel and Coal
Timothy Eaton   Company
Adam Beck Dominion Iron and Steel
Rodolphe Forget La Ligue Nationaliste Canadienne

Analysing the Issues
Answer each of the following questions, which deal with important issues raised in the chapter.

1. What factors, both economic and political, favoured Laurier's plan for a second transcontinental railway?
2. How did the natural resource industries of mining and forestry spur the Canadian economy during the Laurier years?
3. What was the nature of the opposition in Quebec to the rapid pace of industrialization and urbanization in that province?

Questions and Discussions
Think carefully about each of the following questions and discuss the issues they raise.

1. The dramatic development of new railway lines during Laurier's time in office was a key factor in the economic boom of the time. Yet these same railways were built on such a shaky financial base that by 1923 the government had to move in to take them over. Did Laurier manage the railway issue well or poorly? What alternative choices might he have made? Explain your answers.
2. American investment in Canada increased dramatically during the first decade of the twentieth century. What were the advantages and disadvantages of this development? In light of your answers, do you think the Canadian government today should encourage greater American investment in Canada?

5

THE UNDERSIDE OF PROSPERITY

By 1910, Winnipeg's North End, the "foreign quarter," was bulging with poor people, mostly recent immigrants. The newcomers had unfamiliar names, difficult for English- and French-speaking people to pronounce and impossible to spell. Even canvassers for Winnipeg's City Directory gave up and listed many of them merely as "foreigners." Since immigrants were still pouring into the city, almost everyone in the North End took in roomers.

For many people, living conditions in the North End were horrible. Michael Yakoff, a Ruthenian who earned twelve dollars a month as a caretaker, lived there in three rooms with his wife and child, paying eight dollars a month for rent. The Yakoffs took in roomers, and little Pieter Yakoff, age eight, brought in a few extra pennies scavenging for wood in the alleyways. Typical of the district's rooming houses was that of Mrs. Chudek on Austin Street. She had thirty-two people huddled into rooms that might be expected to sleep seven. Once she was hauled into court and scolded by the local magistrate. "People are supposed to live like human beings and not like hogs," he declared. "In your house there was not space for a dog, let alone a man. Besides being overcrowded the place was abominably filthy." To the Reverend Charles Gordon, a staunch defender of Anglo-Saxon values, the North End was a horrid slum, "a howling chaos . . . an endless grey expanse of mouldering ruin . . . ."

Writing under the pen-name "Ralph Connor," the Rev. Charles Gordon was the author of several popular novels.

The Reverend James Shaver Woodsworth, a young Methodist minister and superintendent of All People's Mission, was one of the few living in the North End by choice. In 1908 he surveyed the conditions around him and aptly observed: "True prosperity cannot be measured by the volume of trade and bank clearings. It consists in the social and moral welfare of the people." Winnipeg's North End seemed untouched by the country's prosperity. How could this be?

Laissez-Faire Liberalism

The extent and tempo of material growth between 1896 and 1911 were a source of genuine pride for Sir Wilfrid Laurier and his government. But the social problems which grew out of rapid industrialization and "open door" immigration were not a major concern of Laurier Liberalism. Laurier's *laissez-faire* principles and his respect for provincial rights did not incline him towards any serious intervention in the free market economy which spawned the problems. Likewise, Laurier was proud of the successes of his immigration policy and loath to recognize its unattractive side-effects. When confronted by native-born Canadians concerned about the flood of new immigrants, he reacted defensively. Urban overcrowding and poverty and the "Canadianization" of "foreigners" were problems which would take care of themselves.

Opposite page: Almost every Canadian city had its slum area where poor families, many of them recent immigrants, lived crowded together in one or two dingy, dilapidated rooms. In Toronto, it was known as "the Ward."

Laurier's skills and experience had equipped him to deal with the problems of an older, quieter, more agrarian Canada whose people almost all came from either British or French backgrounds. His expertise was not of much help when he was forced to address the challenges of a newer, multi-ethnic industrialized society. Being a French-Canadian leader with roots in Quebec, which was very jealous of its provincial rights, he was also reluctant to try to extend the powers of the federal government into social fields as they were considered the preserve of the provinces. As a result Laurier and his brand of Liberalism seemed indifferent to the living conditions and concerns of large segments of Canadian society.

Poverty in an Age of Plenty

Canadian cities experienced an explosion of growth in the Laurier years. As industries expanded, workers were drawn from overseas or from rural areas to fill places in the factories, on building projects or in service industries. The pace and extent of urbanization changed the character of Canadian society. Canada's two largest cities, Montreal and Toronto, more than doubled in size. Every city from Montreal westward took on the character of a boomtown. The population of Winnipeg and Vancouver increased fivefold, while Calgary, Edmonton, Regina and Saskatoon burst forth as cities from almost nothing. All of the cities—old and new—had areas of wide, tree-lined streets where the wealthy lived in spacious elegant houses with well-planned lawns and gardens. And all had an area of slums where the poor crowded together in flimsy shacks or tenement housing without running water, sewers or adequate heating.

Slum conditions were nothing new, but their persistence and growth in the midst of plenty was unsettling. Fortunately, the Laurier-era prosperity, while it did not reach all levels of society, did produce a few progressive-minded social reformers with the leisure time and incentive to consider the plight of the poor. Canadians became more aware of poverty and social conditions in the cities than at any time in their past.

A Gathering Urban Crisis

The horrors of poverty in a Canadian city at the turn of the century were graphically illustrated in a study published in 1897 by Herbert B. Ames, a reform-minded Montreal businessman. Entitled *The City below the Hill*, the study focused on the working-class districts stretching from the foot of Mount Royal to the riverfront and revealed some shocking facts. The annual death rate for the city of Montreal in 1895 was twenty-five per thousand, higher than for London, Paris, Rome, Boston or New York. In the worst sections of the town, the death rate reached as

Population 1901

Montreal	328 172
Toronto	209 892
Quebec	68 840
Ottawa	59 928
Hamilton	52 634
Winnipeg	42 340
Halifax	40 832
Saint John	40 711
Vancouver	29 432
Calgary	4 392
Edmonton	4 176
Regina	2 249
Saskatoon	113

Population 1911

Montreal	490 504
Toronto	381 833
Winnipeg	136 035
Vancouver	120 847
Ottawa	87 062
Hamilton	81 869
Quebec	78 710
Halifax	46 619
Calgary	43 704
Saint John	42 511
Edmonton	31 064
Regina	30 213
Saskatoon	12 004

high as thirty-five people per thousand. An untreated water supply, the sale of untested, unpasteurized milk, and the widespread use of outdoor pit privies crowded together in tiny backyards were only some of the reasons for the high death rate. Intestinal diseases were common, especially in infants and small children. To make matters worse, the city and provincial governments spent only tiny amounts on public health, welfare and education, leaving private charities to deal with the poor. "The citizens of Montreal," Ames bluntly stated, "should, for a time, cease discussing the slums of London, the beggars of Paris and the tenement house evils of New York and endeavour to learn something about . . . the conditions present in their midst."

The situation in Toronto was not all that much better. Toronto's working class remained almost untouched by the benefits of prosperity. Wages rose slightly, but the standard of living of the industrial worker did not improve since prices rose as much or more. Average working hours dropped from ten to nine hours a day, but most workers still toiled in dirty, poorly ventilated, dimly lit and unsanitary factories and workshops. Toronto's tenement house district, "The Ward," was a dirty, rat-infested, unhealthy place to live. The state of public health was revealed by Toronto's death and infant mortality rates, which were somewhat lower that Montreal's but no cause for civic pride.

What had caused the social decay? In the case of Toronto, the shortage of housing played a major role. Toronto's population jumped from 181 000 to 382 000 between 1891 and 1911. Construction could simply not keep up with the increased demand. Thousands of those flooding into the city and looking for lodgings were European immigrants unable to afford the prices decent housing commanded in such circumstances. As a result, decaying older neighbourhoods degenerated rapidly into ramshackle rooming house districts. According to a Toronto relief officer, the situation was so bad in 1904 that there was "scarcely a vacant house fit to live in," and even "respectable people had to live in stables, tents, old cars, sheds (others in damp cellars), where we would not put a valued animal, let alone a human being."

Winnipeg was a breeding ground for social discontent. Nowhere was the line dividing rich and poor as sharply drawn. The well-to-do of the South End and the prosperous middle class and skilled working class of the central city—mostly of British background—were separated by massive CPR rail yards from the low-income, unskilled, largely immigrant working class of the North End. Many North Enders agreed with J.S. Woodsworth that the basic cause of their grinding poverty was the low wages paid by employers unwilling to share their growing profits with working people.

Vancouver suffered from a somewhat special set of condi-

Cost of Living
In 1900, the Dominion Department of Labour calculated that the cost of food, laundry starch, fuel, lighting and rent of a six-room dwelling was $490 a year. Ten years later, these selected items in the family budget had increased more than 30 percent to $640 a year.

Incomes in the Montreal Building Trades
Average income for five categories of building trade craftsmen who were heads of families in 1911 came to $711 per year. Only the highest paid category, trainmen, earned enough to place a family above the poverty line without the assistance of a second wage earner.

Winnipeg—the "right"
and the "wrong" side of
the tracks.

tions. As the principal urban centre in British Columbia, the city served as a kind of Mecca for workers in the western resource industries during the off-season or when they were fired or laid off in hard times. Although other cities were worse off, Vancouver's biggest problem was providing relief for the jobless single men who flooded into the city at various times in the year.

Vancouver's difficulties with the unemployed came to a head during the short recession of 1907-08. The construction boom in the city suddenly halted and a host of hinterland industries shut down. "A month ago," reported the magazine *Westward Ho!* in December 1907, "everything was booming. Now nearly all native industries have closed down. Smelting, lumbering and logging are at a complete standstill, and mining has been reduced by at least two-thirds." The economic downturn sent thousands of transients scurrying for aid. Volunteer agencies like the Salvation Army simply could not cope, and the civic authorities were forced to introduce a "work-for-relief" program. Here, at least, transient labourers would not be allowed to starve.

Social workers and reformers in all major Canadian cities warned of a gathering urban crisis. In Toronto, the Reverend H.S. Magee charged that the deplorable housing conditions were the result of "criminal" carelessness. Dr. Helen MacMurchy, a Toronto school medical inspector, went even further in a blistering 1912 report on infant death.

> The Canadian city is still essentially uncivilized—it is neither properly paved nor drained, nor supplied with water fit to drink, nor equipped with any adequate health organization . . . . After ages will wonder at the stupidity of Government and a people which takes so much trouble to bring in immigrants from every corner of Europe . . . and, for sheer lack of public thought, lets its own Canadian babies die in quite unnecessary holocaust, and for sheer lack of civic organization, allows even the labourers it has brought over to be decimated by enteric fever due to a contaminated water supply.

Spearheads of Urban Reform

Much of the demand for reform before the turn of the century was stirred up by the "people's press"—a new crop of popular newspapers like the Montreal *Star*, the Toronto *World* and the Ottawa *Journal*. Fiercely independent in politics and sensational in tone, they bombarded the public with facts and stories detailing the sorry state of Canadian cities. Indeed, for some of these papers, advocating urban reform and attacking the civic establishment became a favourite way of boosting circulation.

Before long, a new breed of experts replaced the journalists as the spearheads of reform. Herbert Ames, the businessman who had written *The City Below the Hill*, carried his reforming zeal into Montreal politics in 1898. As alderman and then as chairman of the municipal board of health from 1900 to 1904, he worked energetically to solve some of the city's urgent health problems. In the field of social work, J.J. Kelso, a one-time Toronto journalist, reached national prominence as a strong advocate of child welfare and organized Children's Aid societies throughout the country. A former journalist and Quebec provincial cabinet minister, G.A. Nantel, proposed a grandiose scheme of civic reform and beautification for Montreal in 1910, based upon the experience of Paris. And in 1911 J.S. Woodsworth's book *My Neighbour* appeared, outlining living conditions in Canada's cities and making an emotional appeal for reform.

Much of the spirit of reform grew out of an emerging form of active Christianity known as the "social gospel," a movement that originated in Britain and the United States and spread into Canada. Its leaders, men like the Reverend Salem Bland, were mostly drawn from the Protestant churches. They preached that Christ's message was a social gospel, that it was the Christian's duty to make people's lives better here on earth, before saving their souls for heaven. This reform impulse led Christian activists such as Miss Sara Libby Carson to found Canadian settlement houses, homes ministering to the needs of the urban poor and destitute immigrants.

Some social gospel advocates, notably J.S. Woodsworth and the Reverend Dr. D.M. Ramsey of Ottawa, came to link the Christian mission with socialism, a political philosophy which extended into economic areas the "Christian doctrine of human brotherhood." Every Christian, it was said, was his brother's keeper.

These reform leaders did not work alone. Their efforts to arouse the public and to initiate reform were supported by a variety of voluntary organizations, many of which dated back to the 1880s. Older Christian bodies like the Women's Christian Temperance Union, the Young Men's Christian Association, and the Salvation Army stepped up their crusades to rid society of vice, crime and poverty. They were joined by the established churches, which by the 1890s were sponsoring relief agencies and charity drives, mission houses, social settlements and later social service councils. To one astonished Montreal observer, it seemed as if people had been seized by some irresistible urge to "save mankind." Such groups as the Civic Art Guild of Toronto and the City Improvement League of Montreal launched campaigns to clean up and beautify the cities—to extend sewer and water systems and other services to poorer neighbourhoods, to provide

For the Indians of western Canada, the influx of settlers meant stricter confinement to reservations and the loss of the last remnants of their cherished freedom. Some adjusted and became successful farmers, but most found it difficult if not impossible to make the transition to an agricultural way of life. The result on most reserves was a way of life characterized by poverty, disease and a general sense of hopelessness.

more parks, playgrounds and public libraries, so that not only the well-to-do could enjoy the benefits of fresh air and open green spaces and good books.

After 1901, the reform idea gained strength in city politics. Reform-minded politicians organized the Union of Canadian Municipalities and urged city governments to take control of the privately owned services and utilities operating in urban areas.

Franchises issued to private telephone, street railway and electric light companies had created utilities free from municipal control. The streets of the major Canadian cities were a tangle of street car tracks and wires, telephone poles and wires, electricity poles and wires. City councils by the turn of the century had become locked in ongoing battles with private electrical, telephone and street railway companies over rights-of-way, service and rates. Reform-minded politicians and businessmen argued that public ownership could improve efficiency and place these services under more business-like management.

However, reform measures such as public ownership of utilities and city beautification were not necessarily implemented for

idealistic purposes. While they might satisfy the desire of reformers for a more efficient management and broader distribution of the province's resources, they frequently gave business interests a greater opportunity to mould city development. Some improvements were made in health standards, public housing, workmen's compensation, pensions and child welfare, but the social reformers failed to institute changes that might threaten to "clog the wheels" of economic progress.

The Limited Federal Role

In the Canada of the Laurier years the federal government assumed little responsibility for social welfare or the management of private utilities. Assistance for the urban and rural poor came largely from local and provincial governments. But the creation of the Canadian Commission of Conservation in 1909 under Laurier's former Interior minister, Clifford Sifton, at least seemed to provide a modest base for future involvement. Though only a federal advisory body, the commission did initiate studies and investigations into resource problems, public health, town planning and housing. Because social problems were seen as an exclusively provincial responsibility under the British North America Act, however, no serious actions were taken by the Laurier government. Widespread urban poverty and blight persisted. Corporations and the wealthy classes were left to be the true leaders and beneficiaries of national economic progress.

Times of Trouble

Like the country's urban problems, labour unrest grew in intensity at a time when Canada's economy was booming. The mines, mills and factories were belching smoke and filling orders, but prosperity did not seem to reach the bunkhouses or the city slums. From the late 1890s into the new century prices rose dramatically and wages lagged behind. While men of capital amassed large fortunes in industry and commerce, workers had to scrap with employers for a share of the growing economic pie. The result was a seething discontent among working people that often erupted into industrial conflict and even violence.

Canada's rapid economic expansion thus brought dramatic changes in relations between capital and labour. Giant industrial corporations had grown to dominate large segments of the economy. In both the East and the West, in city and in country, the rush of new immigrants had driven up land values and depressed wages. Periodic, short-term economic collapses had struck the nation's mines, mills, factories and railways, creating bouts of unemployment, deprivation and human suffering. Confronted with such conditions, a growing number of working people turned to trade unions for protection and security.

The federal government established residential schools where Indian children were expected to learn the ways of the majority. Unfortunately, those who did were seldom accepted into the new society developing on the prairie, and all too often their schooling and new ways made them outsiders among their own people as well.

Gompers's Shadow

The new spurt of union activity completely transformed the country's fledgling labour movement. Although Canada's small and scattered unions had formed a national organization, the Trades and Labour Congress of Canada (TLC), in 1886, they represented only a tiny minority of workers. Now a new brand of trade unionism swept into the country from the United States.

The American Federation of Labor (AFL), headed by Samuel Gompers, had been organized in 1886 to counter the growth of American corporate power by establishing larger, more centralized trade unions—one national union for each trade and craft. Within a few years, the AFL had succeeded in winning significant benefits for its members.

Concerned about the possibility that employers might look north of the border for cheaper labour, the AFL launched an aggressive organizing drive in Canada from 1898 to 1902. Under Sam Gompers's watchful eye, John Flett of Hamilton and other union organizers established a network of craft union locals throughout Ontario and in every one of the Maritime provinces. Unions, once confined to the skilled workers in such industries as the railways, printing and construction, were firmly established in the metal trades, the garment industry, woodworking, and extended to some unskilled classes of railway workers. More than seven hundred locals were chartered in the four-year period, raising union membership from some twenty thousand to more than seventy thousand across Canada.

Of course, none of this happened without opposition from several quarters. Employers were hostile in principle and made rousing appeals to anti-American feelings in an effort to undermine the growing AFL support—in spite of the fact that many were, themselves, American. Some unionists were more genuinely nationalistic and advocated the creation of a similar but independent Canadian organization. In Quebec, elements of the Catholic clergy actively opposed the entry of AFL unions and began organizing their own *syndicats catholiques*, based on French-Canadian customs and closely tied to the Church.

Nonetheless, at the Trades and Labour Congress Convention of 1902 in Berlin (Kitchener), Ontario, Canadian union delegates from 102 organizations endorsed the AFL's brand of international unionism, voting to expel any group that tried to compete with an international union. Expelled unions formed their own organization, the Canadian Federation of Labour (CFL), but for many years to come, Canadian workers would prefer to support American-based unions.

Not all trade unionists saw the craft-based AFL (and CFL) type unions as the fighting edge of the labour movement, however. No matter how hard such unions might work to preserve

skilled crafts, machine production was relentlessly replacing them. Skilled craftsmen were becoming an ever smaller part of the labour force, and their unions seemed unlikely to be very useful to the armies of unskilled workers who performed the repetitive, mechanical tasks in factories or the heavy labour in mining, lumber and railway construction camps. The Western Federation of Miners (WFM) and a few other American unions that had had to fight particularly hard battles against ruthless employers believed in organizing on a much broader base. Some of them were shouting for workers to take more radical political action. Nowhere was this spirit of militant industrial unionism more evident than in the mines, mills and railway camps of British Columbia.

Radical trade unionism came to Canada in the 1890s when giant American corporations opened mines in the Kootenay and Boundary districts of British Columbia. Experienced hard-rock miners, mostly American-born and card-carrying members of the Western Federation of Miners, moved freely into the province. When the CPR built a new line through the Crow's Nest Pass in

Unlike most unions of the day, the Western Federation of Miners welcomed workers of every background.

1897, more mines opened and the influence of the WFM further expanded. In the Rossland strike of 1901, the WFM local of smeltermen was crushed when the companies imported strike-breakers. Labour leaders appealed to their members for political action. Workers in the interior and on Vancouver Island responded in 1902 by electing two union men running as socialists to the British Columbia Legislature—the first such members elected anywhere in the British Empire.

The Wobblies

One of the most colourful episodes of labour radicalism in British Columbia in the years before 1914 was the dramatic rise and fall of the IWW, the International Workers of the World, nicknamed "The Wobblies." Formed in 1905 at Chicago to fight Sam Gompers's brand of "craft unionism," the IWW sought to organize all industrial workers into One Big Union that could then stop work in a great general strike to bring about radical change. After surviving a serious internal split in 1907, the Wobblies, under the leadership of "Big Bill" Haywood, expanded their aggressive campaign against what they called "the pure and simple-dom"of Gompers's AFL into British Columbia.

In the years after 1908 the Wobblies gained much support among unskilled, itinerant workers, including loggers, longshoremen and railway construction workers on the Canadian Northern and Grand Trunk Pacific lines. Unlike the AFL and other craft unions, the IWW welcomed "blanketstiffs" and transient workers of every immigrant background. By 1912 the Wobblies boasted twelve union locals, some five thousand members and claimed the support of nearly 40 percent of all railway construction workers. The union won respect from labour for its courageous fights for free speech in Victoria, Edmonton and other western towns. Yet the idea of organizing transient labour proved futile. When the railway construction boom ended, the IWW disintegrated as a force in western Canada.

The Struggles of the Provincial Workmen's Association

Compared to the turbulent industrial warfare on the West Coast, the labour scene in the Maritimes seemed tranquil. Only in Nova Scotia was there a firmly established labour organization—the Provincial Workmen's Association (PWA)—and it was more concerned with survival than with militancy.

Since its founding in 1879, the PWA had favoured negotiations over strikes. It had won the grudging respect of Nova Scotia mine operators and, for its workers, the right to hire "tallymen" to check the company weigh scales and the best safety legislation in the world at that time. In spite of these gains, the future of the PWA always seemed in jeopardy. Mines in the province were marginal and still dreadfully unsafe. The union survived periodic raids by more militant labour organizations, but was torn by internal strife. Then, to make matters worse, the small mining companies it had been dealing with were gradually taken over by the Dominion Steel and Coal Company, a giant combine with interests in lumber and shipping.

A showdown with Dominion Coal and Steel was not long in coming. Under John Moffatt, its new Grand Secretary, the PWA settled its internal differences and became feisty. Departing from its policy of representing only mine workers, it expanded into smelting by taking in workers at Dominion's Sydney mill. The outcome of this decision was a disastrous strike in 1904. After a seven-week struggle, most of the mill workers lost their jobs and the PWA was left in a shambles. Dominion Coal and Steel continued to collect union dues for the PWA, but this merely served as a reminder that the company now controlled its very existence.

With the PWA financially broken and virtually impotent, a rival union, the aggressive United Mine Workers of America, attempted a takeover. The UMW, with three hundred thousand members, was the biggest union in the United States and a loyal supporter of the AFL. Both the PWA leadership and Dominion Steel fought to keep this "foreign bully" out, but most of the miners wanted to join the UMW. A long and bitter strike erupted in 1909 and threatened to bring Cape Breton to the brink of civil war. Since many miners lived in company-owned houses, strikers and their families were driven from their dwellings and forced to spend most of the bitter cold winter of 1909-10 huddled in tents on the barren hills overlooking Sydney and Glace Bay. Families were torn apart, friendships destroyed; scores of men were arrested. To guard the mines and protect the strike-breakers, most of Canada's small permanent militia was called in and waited out the same dismal winter in Cape Breton.

The PWA won the 1909-10 skirmish, but lost the larger war. After pouring one million dollars into the strike, the UMW conceded defeat and Dominion Steel signed a new "company-made" contract with the PWA. Support for the UMW simply went underground and, after seven years of tireless union organizing, re-emerged to capture the leadership of the miners' union. By 1918 the PWA had been totally eroded and some eleven thousand Cape Breton miners were virtually absorbed by the UMW international union.

Mackenzie King's Approach to Labour

The Liberal government of Sir Wilfrid Laurier sought to dampen industrial conflict by wooing organized labour. In 1900 a new federal Department of Labour was created under Sir William Mulock to investigate wages and working conditions and, where

Mackenzie King
campaigns for election
in 1908.

possible, to solve disputes between workers and employers. As his
deputy minister, Mulock chose William Lyon Mackenzie King, a
young labour relations specialist with progressive ideas and a
reputation as an investigator of sweatshops. In a further attempt
to win over organized labour, the government appointed Daniel
O'Donoghue and three other prominent trade unionists to government jobs. "If there is an aristocracy in this country," Laurier
told the 1900 TLC convention, "it is an aristocracy of labour to
which all belong."

Apart from the glittering rhetoric, Laurier's only answer to
labour conflict was Mackenzie King. King was a Harvard-trained
labour expert who believed in maintaining industrial peace at all

costs. Business, labour and government, King claimed, could solve any dispute if the facts were revealed and cool heads prevailed. The idea that labour and capital were locked in a death struggle horrified King. Workers and employers needed each other, he insisted, and both sides must be convinced to behave in the public interest.

King's ideas shaped much of federal labour policy. Under his direction, the department attempted conciliation in a series of serious industrial disputes, including the 1902 British Columbia railway strike and a bitter 1906 strike in the Alberta coal mines. The Conciliation Act of 1900 and the Railway Labour Disputes Act of 1903 were two cautious but concrete steps towards a federal role as umpire in labour disputes. Of almost seven hundred disputes in Canada from 1900 to 1907, forty-one were referred to federal conciliators, resulting in thirty-three settlements. Although King's Department claimed to be acting impartially, many of its actions upheld company interests.

In spite of King's initiatives, labour disputes grew more ugly, often spreading beyond the original contenders. The nine-month coal strike in the Lethbridge and Crowsnest Pass districts in 1906 left prairie settlers in danger of freezing to death. That same year, in the Quebec lumber town of Buckingham, the MacLaren Lumber Company fired its striking workers and precipitated a clash which left three dead and many others wounded. Public opinion was horrified. The government must act.

Mackenzie King was ready. What was needed was a law to make both sides wait while the public learned the facts. Then the side that continued the dispute unfairly would feel public anger. The product of King's thinking was enacted by Parliament in 1907: the Industrial Disputes Investigation (IDI) Act.

The IDI Act was heralded as a landmark in progressive labour legislation and earned King international recognition as a conciliation expert. Yet the Act itself did not seem to live up to its billing. While it gave workers with a weak union a chance to state their case, in most instances it hampered unions more than employers. Since no strike was permitted during an investigation, employers could use the time to train replacement workers and build up stock to supply their customers in the event of a work stoppage. Nothing in the Act gave workers the right to join a union or compelled employers to negotiate. And since public opinion was largely shaped by wealthy newspaper owners, it seemed more likely to favour employers than workers.

The IDI Act's severe limitations were revealed in two celebrated strikes. In 1907 a strike by Bell Telephone Company operators in Toronto attracted immense public interest and sympathy because the strikers were women. The dispute was sent to conciliation and eventually settled by a report that merely slapped the

From 1901 to 1913, according to the Labour Gazette, *there were fourteen major strikes in communities from British Columbia to Nova Scotia involving riots, mob violence, property damage, personal injuries and—in two cases—deaths. Eleven of these strikes were controlled—or ended—by the intervention of militia or regular military forces.*

Women and Unions

Women were entering the labour force in ever increasing numbers, giving up their traditional jobs as domestics to join the expanding ranks of female factory workers, secretaries, shop clerks and telephone operators. Relatively few, however, were employed in unionized occupations.

company's wrists, dismissed the operators' demands for wages and recognition, and appeared only after half the women workers had left the company. In the case of the Grand Trunk Railway strike of 1910, the IDI Act worked even more to the benefit of management. Employees followed IDI Act rules and accepted delays in negotiations which cost them job and pension rights, only to discover that the final settlement hardly differed from the position taken by the company.

King's labour legislation helped defuse conflict, but also made strikes much harder to win.

The Right to Combine

The Laurier government's reluctance to intervene was also shown in other areas of the expanding market economy. Even the rise of big business and the great wave of mergers after 1907 was slow to provoke a reaction from Ottawa. Since gaining power in 1896, Laurier had shown little interest in tampering with the protective tariff or in controlling the "combines" nesting under its wing. Noisy public campaigns in the United States against the evils of "trusts" made little impact on Laurier and his ministers. But after 1907 Canada was hit by a wave of "consolidations" and rapidly rising consumer prices. The full force of the merger movement struck in the years 1909 and 1910, when thirty-one combinations were formed worth $290 million, driving hundreds of small Canadian companies out of business. Signs were everywhere that combines and their ruthless price-fixing practices had arrived in Canada.

The merger wave and its attendant problems finally forced the government to take action. It responded in 1910 with legislation introduced by Mackenzie King, who was now Laurier's Minister of Labour. The Combines Investigation Act of 1910 set up machinery to investigate activities in "restraint of trade," but changed little else. In defending the Act, King argued that most mergers promoted economic efficiency and that any further restrictions would slow the pace of industrial expansion. The Act was a "toothless wonder," designed to quiet public criticism without doing any serious damage to corporate interests. It was invoked once, with little effect, against an American shoe machine combine and quietly repealed in 1919.

With its weak anti-combines legislation, the Laurier government almost conceded to businessmen the right to combine. Men of capital proceeded to build bigger industries, eliminate competition and set prices without restraint.

By 1911 Canada was approaching a time of critical national decision. Social strains in Canadian cities, economic troubles between labour and employers, and cultural tensions between French-speaking and English-speaking, Catholic and Protestant, native- and foreign-born Canadians were coming into sharp relief. In Ottawa the federal government was still led by the prime minister of the "sunny ways" of optimism. His approach remained essentially one of *laissez-faire* and non-intervention regardless of the social costs. New versions of Tory policies stressing British-Canadian national loyalties, Anglo-Saxonism in immigration and education and active intervention in economic and social matters seemed to be attracting an increasingly broad measure of support. The political ascendancy of Laurier Liberalism seemed, for the first time, to be threatened.

REVIEW AND DISCUSSION

Key People and Ideas
Explain the importance of each of the following as they are discussed in the chapter.

James Shaver Woodsworth

Herbert B. Ames

Dr. Helen MacMurchy

J.J. Kelso

Sara Libby Carson

Samuel Gompers

"Big Bill" Haywood

John Moffatt

William Lyon Mackenzie King

All People's Mission

The "social gospel"

Canadian Commission of Conservation

Trades and Labour Congress of Canada

Canadian Federation of Labour

"The Wobblies"

Provincial Workmen's Association

Industrial Disputes Investigation Act

Combines Investigation Act

Analysing the Issues
Answer each of the following questions, which deal with important issues raised in the chapter.

1. What were the conditions in Canadian cities which led to the demand for social reform? What factors had led to these conditions?
2. How was religion linked to social reform in Canadian cities in the early years of the twentieth century?
3. What factors led to the growth of the Canadian union movement during the Laurier era?
4. What attempts were made by radical unions to win improved wages and working conditions for unskilled workers?

Question for Discussion
Think carefully about the following question and discuss the issues it raises.

1. What were the strengths and weaknesses of Mackenzie King's approach to labour–management relations? On balance, do you think King's policies represented a realistic way to deal with the problems of industrial relations in Canada? Why or why not?

6

THE FALL FROM GRACE

By 1911 storm clouds appeared to be gathering around Sir Wilfrid Laurier and his government. Canada was confronted with important choices in her relations with Britain, the United States and the world. Memories of the Boer War in South Africa and the Alaska Boundary dispute still lingered in the minds of many Canadians. The Boer War crisis of 1899 had started an ongoing public debate about Canada's proper place in the British Empire. The Alaska Boundary award of 1903 had stimulated nationalistic feelings and aroused latent anti-American attitudes among some Canadians. Was Canada now ready to assume greater autonomy and responsibilities in external relations?

As prime minister, Sir Wilfrid Laurier had been walking a tightrope for fifteen years. He had managed to balance the differing aspirations of the French-speaking and English-speaking Canadian communities, but the fragile harmony of French-English relations—as well as his lease on power—depended on good fortune as well as on his skill at finding compromises and defusing crises. Now this precarious balancing act seemed threatened.

Imperialist sentiment in Canada had been stoked by growing fears of an impending conflict between Britain and Germany. The Dominion itself had been remade by fifteen years of prosperity and rapid economic change. To many French Canadians, and especially to *nationalistes* like Henri Bourassa, Laurier's compromises had led to a series of "sell-outs" to *les Anglais* on issues such as Manitoba schools, the Boer War and the 1905 Autonomy Bills. The day of reckoning seemed to be approaching.

Conflicting Perceptions of Canada's Interests
Throughout the Laurier years, Canada was torn by conflicting ideas on where the nation's interests lay. Steering the Canadian ship of state in such circumstances was a difficult business. In guiding the country's external relations, the Laurier government had to steer a middle course through the shoals of imperial sentiment, French-Canadian nationalism, anti-Americanism, French-English tensions and public concern over the "immigrant problem."

Canada's relations with the United States seemed untroubled on the surface. The strong national feelings aroused by the Alaska Boundary decision had subsided, and steps had been taken in the intervening years to solve other problems. Yet beneath the public display of goodwill there remained a lingering suspicion of the United States. The bruised feelings of 1903 had not healed completely—and even the smallest sign of American continental ambitions was enough to conjure up fears of Manifest Destiny in Canada.

On the question of imperial relations, Canada was a house

Opposite page: Surrounded by Union Jacks and symbols of western prosperity, Sir Wilfrid Laurier addresses a Moose Jaw crowd during the 1911 election campaign.

divided. The Boer War crisis had pointed up the fact that Canada's existing relationship with the Empire was unsatisfactory to both English- and French-speaking Canadians. To many English Canadians Laurier's policy had relegated Canada to the role of a colony aiding the mother country in the South African war. Colonel George T. Denison, George M. Parkin and other imperialists considered Laurier's position a disgrace: Canada should have made a larger contribution and asserted her equality as a nation within a united British Empire. But not all Canadians felt the strength of loyalty to Britain evident in much of English Canada. To them, the defence of Britain's far-flung empire was none of Canada's concern. French-Canadian leaders such as Bourassa and Armand Lavergne professed loyalty to Canada first and a willingness to defend only that portion of the Empire which was the "homeland" of Canadians.

"The Nationalists of Quebec today," Lavergne told the Military Institute in 1910, "are willing and ready to give their last drop of blood for the defence of the British flag and British institutions in this country."

To some extent, the deep misunderstanding between French and English in Canada was a product of living in "two solitudes." In early twentieth-century Canada little social or cultural interplay existed between the two communities, except in the field of politics. Even in the city of Montreal, where the French and English lived side by side, each group went its own way with little concern for the other. In the English enclaves of Westmount and McGill University, the bourgeois classes buzzed with the imperialist ideas of Andrew Macphail and Stephen Leacock, almost oblivious to the *nationaliste* views expounded by Henri Bourassa, Armand Lavergne and Olivar Asselin.

Lord Minto, the Governor General and an astute and sympathetic observer of Canadian society, described the state of affairs in a letter to his brother in 1902: "Society there (in Montreal) is most peculiar and difficult, full of cliques and petty jealousies, and the racial division in society absolutely distinct. I am really ashamed of the narrowness of the Britisher—he taboos the French entirely—he chooses to say that they are disloyal—and practically has nothing to do with them, and we found the leaders of society of both races unacquainted with each other."

Aside from French-English tensions, many native-born Canadians were expressing concern about the impact of Canada's thousands of new immigrants on the fabric of Canadian society. A major worry was that new immigrant groups seemed unmoved by patriotic appeals for imperial unity. This deep-felt concern led some Canadian imperialists to become immigration restrictionists, and others to advocate rapid Canadianization of the children of recent immigrants through a national school system.

Confronted with these conflicting perceptions of Canada's interests, Sir Wilfrid Laurier and his government attempted to steer a cautious middle course in relation with the outside world. The divisive Boer War crisis of 1899 had served as a warning.

Laurier's policy was designed to avert repetitions of such a crisis. It was a policy of compromise, which ranged from a defence of the *status quo* to slow, halting steps along the path to Dominion autonomy.

Laurier himself was aware that it was an unheroic policy. Answering a critic in late 1909, he pointed out the difficulties of the government's position: "We are British subjects, but we are an autonomous nation; we are divided into provinces, we are divided into races, and out of these confused elements the man at the head of affairs has to sail the ship onwards, and to do this safely it is not always the ideal policy from the point of view of pure idealism which ought to prevail, but the policy which can appeal on the whole to all sections of the community."

Canadian Control and the Military

Laurier's cautious approach was clearly exemplified in his response to a growing feeling of militarism in English Canada. As prosperity gave Canadians optimism, self-confidence and a renewed desire to cut a figure in the world, militarist thinking began to assert itself throughout British Canada. Prominent Canadian imperialist writers like Andrew Macphail and Charles Mair spoke of enthusiasm for war as a tonic to cure the ills of materialism and self-indulgence. Growing support for ideas such as patriotism, order and discipline was amply reflected in Canada's rising cadet

While politicians wrangled, Alexander Graham Bell and a couple of young Canadians, Casey Baldwin and John McCurdy, were making aviation history. In 1909 they produced the *Silver Dart* and made the first powered flight in the British Empire. Seen here is their *Baddeck I* being readied for a demonstration to army staff in 1910. Unfortunately, both it and the *Silver Dart* were damaged during the demonstration and the army decided to stay on the ground.

movement. Between 1900 and 1913, the militia expanded and the number of boys in cadet training reached over forty thousand.

Laurier responded to the growth of militaristic sentiment in predictable fashion. To him, the spirit of Canadian self-confidence suggested the need for greater national control over local military forces. Yet even here the initiative seemed to come from Britain. Certainly this was the case in the 1904-05 decision to withdraw British naval forces from the Canadian ports of Halifax, Nova Scotia, and Esquimalt, British Columbia, and to transfer control over the garrisons from Britain to Canada. The transfer owed more to Britain's desire to meet a growing German naval threat by reorganizing the Royal Navy than to Laurier's insistence on Canada assuming its full responsibilities as a self-governing Dominion. Indeed, if Canada had declined to garrison the ports, the British War Office and Admiralty planned simply to abandon them.

The most irritating defence issue was the role of the GOC, the British-appointed General Officer commanding the Canadian Militia. The GOC's position under the Militia Act, last revised in 1883, was a peculiar one. Though officially subordinate to the Minister of Militia, he was charged with the dual task of maintaining the imperial military connection and promoting an efficient Canadian militia force.

The Fight for Militia Reform

The imperial goals and military objectives of the GOC had led to a series of clashes with Laurier and his government. First there was a lengthy public row between General Edward Hutton, the GOC appointed in 1898, and the Minister of Militia, Sir Frederick Borden, over Canada's role in the Boer War and over the need for militia reform. This led to Hutton's recall in 1900, a move that was thinly camouflaged as a summons to serve in South Africa. Later one of Hutton's successors, the Earl of Dundonald, who became commander in July 1902, issued a damning report on Liberal interference with the militia and ran into similar problems. "If the General commanding the militia has advice to tender," Laurier snapped in the House of Commons, "it is not his right—I say it deliberately—to offer advice to the public, but it is his duty to offer it to the minister, and for that policy the minister shall be responsible."

Sir Frederick Borden moved toward militia reform, but at a slow, measured speed. Of his proposals to upgrade the militia, one that brought the controversy to a head was an amendment to the Militia Act opening up the command to Canadian officers. This measure raised the ire of GOC Dundonald and Governor General Lord Minto, who feared that the post would go to "some utterly incompetent public favourite or political supporter." The

A Taste of Militarism
The Canadian Boy Scout movement, which had ten thousand members by 1910, emphasized forms of military drill and physical exercise. Lord Baden-Powell, the movement's founder, saw scouting as a more effective and thorough preparation for soldiering than traditional regimental drill and cadet training.

Governor General appealed to Britain and secured a delay, but Borden pressed on and added to his reforms a plan to establish a council of senior militia officers. At this point Dundonald made the mistake of going public with his opposition. This was conduct that the Laurier government obviously could not accept—nor Lord Minto condone. A blunt message from the War Office brought Dundonald back to England. To a large throng of Ottawa well-wishers who waved him farewell, he shouted dramatically, "Men of Canada, keep both hands on the Union Jack."

Dundonald's recall may have stilled the controversy, but many retained the impression that the country's defence needs ranked low on the government's list of priorities. In fact, the Laurier years were times of impressive military reform. Modern arms were purchased or built, including the ambitious, if ill-conceived, Ross Rifle. A new Militia Council was created in 1904; military camps such as Petawawa were purchased; and Canadians took responsibility for the naval bases at Halifax and Esquimalt. The militia grew from 28 000 to almost 50 000, and training camps were now conducted annually instead of in alternate years. As Minister of Militia, Sir Frederick Borden also won a larger share of government revenues for defence and greatly improved the preparedness of the Canadian forces.

The Imperial Defence Question
In his dealings with Britain, Laurier had always been wary of

Whatever doubts most Canadians might have about airplanes, they were taking to automobiles with enthusiasm—more enthusiasm, it would seem, than expertise.

committing Canada to closer imperial relations. Since the 1897 Imperial Conference, he had resisted all appeal for formal imperial federation and had seemed to accept the vaguely defined *status quo* relationship among the members of the Empire. While always ready with an eloquent expression of warmth toward Britain and the Empire, Laurier made it clear that the Dominion's responsibilities within that association would be decided in Canada, by Canadians. It was the kind of attitude that infuriated British imperialists like Premier L.S. Jamieson of the Cape Colony in South Africa and British poet Rudyard Kipling. Imperial enthusiast Lord Milner spoke for many when he complained that Laurier seemed to favour "the present Colonial position with the prospect of future separation" over a "position of national equality with the United Kingdom."

For a short time after the Boer War, the issue faded somewhat in importance. After 1905, however, an escalating naval rivalry between Britain and Germany focused attention once again on matters of imperial defence. In 1906 the Royal Navy produced H.M.S. *Dreadnought*, a super battleship that gave its name to a whole class of ships. She mounted ten 12-inch (30 cm) guns, was driven by turbines and was almost as long as a soccer field. *Dreadnought* suddenly made all older battleships obsolete and touched off a fierce naval-building race. Britain and Germany were already locked in a naval race when news reports in 1909 revealed a secret German dreadnought construction program. Near panic broke out in England. Cries arose for the immediate construction of eight dreadnoughts to ensure that Britain maintained her naval superiority.

The naval race with Germany imposed heavy costs on the British taxpayer. A public outcry in 1909 forced British Prime Minister Henry Campbell-Bannerman's Liberal government to double its naval construction program. The government, already committed to large new expenditures on special programs, found the increased naval costs too much to bear. The colonies must be asked to help.

Response came quickly from Australia and New Zealand. In Australia, the government of Alfred Deakin committed itself to rebuilding its navy. New Zealand, ever the most loyal colony, enthusiastically offered Britain the gift of one dreadnought—and a second if required. Against this background Canada confronted the problem of naval defence.

Laurier and his government were caught in a difficult position. They were committed to developing a naval defence policy, but firmly opposed to any purely financial contribution to Britain. The introduction of a Conservative resolution in the House of Commons calling for Canada to bear her "proper share" of imperial naval costs finally forced Laurier's hand. In March 1909 he put forward a motion so general in nature that it passed unanimously. Canada went on record as supporting the principle of a Canadian navy, but the wording of the resolution left open the possibility of a temporary "emergency" contribution to Britain. Deep internal divisions between French- and English-speaking Canadians, and within the two political parties, were papered over in a show of unity.

The "Tin Pot Navy"

The uneasy consensus on naval policy was soon broken by Laurier's Naval Service Bill. This piece of legislation, introduced in January 1910, provided for the establishment of a Canadian navy composed of five cruisers and six destroyers. The navy was to be placed under Canadian command, but in time of war and with the consent of Parliamant, it could be placed at the disposal of Britain.

Laurier's Naval Bill was a perfect reflection of his ambiguous position on Canada's status within the Empire. "When Britain is at war," Laurier insisted, "Canada is at war." At the same time, the Naval Bill and Laurier's speeches made it clear that the extent of Canadian participation in any imperial war would be decided in Parliament, by Canada alone. It was primarily a political ploy, designed to keep the Liberal party united and to drive a wedge into the gathering opposition forces.

It was humourist Stephen Leacock, then better known as a political economist, who first labelled Laurier's proposed Canadian fleet a "Tin Pot Navy." It was an inspired phrase and Conservatives used it for all it was worth in the ensuing campaign.

This familiar strategy almost worked. Laurier's announcement of the Naval Bill produced some temporary confusion among the Conservative opposition under Robert L. Borden. Influenced by his English-Canadian supporters, who derided whatever assistance Laurier's "Tin Pot Navy" might provide to the British Admiralty as woefully inadequate, Borden began to advocate a direct financial contribution as the only effective way of aiding Britain in a time of dire need. His few French-speaking followers, led by F.D. Monk, opposed both the idea of a financial contribution and Laurier's announced policy. The issue seemed about to create a serious split in Conservative ranks. Instead it provided the Tories with an unlikely ally: Henri Bourassa.

After resigning his seat, Bourassa had thrown his energies into Quebec politics in an effort to dislodge Laurier's provincial allies. His campaigns against the Liberal provincial government of Lomer Gouin strengthened his associations with provincial Conservatives who saw in Bourassa the chance to rebuild their party in Quebec. The naval question provided the occasion to cement the new-found alliance.

In joining the outcry against the Naval Service Bill, Bourassa claimed that the creation of a Canadian navy would draw Canada into the trap of European militarism. In January 1910, when Laurier first announced the Naval Bill, Bourassa launched a new

Henri Bourassa. Writing
in connection with the
naval issue in July 1910,
Bourassa satirized
Laurier's policy of
compromise. The first
thing Sir Wilfrid would
do on reaching the
Gates of Paradise,
Bourassa predicted,
would be "to propose an
honourable compromise
between the good God
and Satan."

French-Canadian nationalist newspaper, *Le Devoir*, with a devastating indictment of the naval policy. Later in the same year he stirred public passions with an electrifying address to the Twelfth Eucharistic Congress of the Roman Catholic Church assembled in Montreal. His eloquent defence of the French language within the Catholic Church won him a hero's applause as the Congress paraded through the streets of Montreal. Further signs of the growing influence of Bourassa appeared when a Liberal was upset by a *nationaliste* candidate in a November 1910 by-election in the riding of Drummond-Arthabaska. The naval issue had cost the Liberals Laurier's old riding and opened the first real chink in Sir Wilfrid's armour. Laurier's hold on Quebec seemed to be crumbling.

Diplomatic Changes Within the North Atlantic Triangle

As international tensions mounted between Britain and Germany, the British sought to strengthen their friendship with the United States. Diplomatic relations between Britain and her North Atlantic triangle partners, the United States and Canada, were aimed at promoting and enlarging Anglo-American friendship. Soothing the wounds inflicted on Canada by the Alaska decision of 1903 and settling a series of older issues between Canada and the United States loomed large on the diplomatic agenda.

The *rapprochement* between Britain and the United States had an important, tranquilizing effect on Canadian-American relations. In a minor "diplomatic revolution" the key players changed: Lord Grey came to Rideau Hall as Governor General, Elihu Root took over the U.S. State Department and James Bryce became British ambassador in Washington. The result was a new era of friendship and collaboration. Almost overnight, Canadian bitterness over the Alaskan affair subsided. Resistance, indecision and endless delays gave way to a feverish "cleaning of the slate" in Canadian-American relations. Signalling the new attitude in Ottawa, Laurier told the House of Commons in 1907 that "we can never conceive of a war between us, or of a war between Great Britain and the United States. We mean to settle all our difficulties with that nation by peaceful means, by diplomatic action, by negotiation but never by war."

The renewed Canadian-American friendship found concrete expression in two major developments. After more than a year of diplomatic manoeuvering and skilful negotiating, a Boundary Waters Treaty was signed in 1909 with the United States. The Treaty not only settled a host of Great Lakes boundary disputes, but also established a permanent International Joint Commission. This body has served as the model for resolving numerous other contentious bilateral issues in the twentieth century. Also in 1909, the Canadian government created a Department of External Affairs so that Canadians would have their own information-gathering and administrative organization, independent of the Colonial Office in London. Its real value, as Lord Grey saw it, was to shorten the diplomatic road between Ottawa and Washington.

The Revival of Reciprocity

A major effect of the new spirit in Canadian-American relations was the revival of discussions of the trade question. In early 1910 the issue was raised by the administration of President William H. Taft, which approached Sir Wilfrid Laurier with the totally unexpected offer of a new reciprocity agreement. Laurier and his government were caught very much by surprise. Having been politically damaged in the past by the reciprocity issue, the Laurier Liberals reacted with understandable hesitation. It sounded too good to be true.

Laurier decided to support reciprocity with the United States. Practical political considerations were involved as well as his own conviction that lower tariffs would prove advantageous to both Canada and the United States. In the summer of 1910, he made a tour of the prairies and British Columbia and found farmers clamouring for tariff reductions and reciprocity wherever he stopped. Later, after reciprocity negotiations were actually underway, a large and aggressive group of organized farmers descended on Ottawa with similar requests. Laurier may also have calculated that opening the American market to farm produce might restore his sagging political support in rural Quebec. Or he may have concluded that his government needed a bold and dramatic new policy after almost fifteen uninterrupted years in office.

Maintaining good relations with the United States was of primary importance to the prime minister, and he was reluctant to jeopardize them by rebuffing Washington's overture. Veiled threats from the Americans to impose heavier duties upon Canada if the Laurier government did not agree to lower tariffs also served as an inducement. Only after negotiations had begun in November 1910 did Finance Minister W.S. Fielding and other Canadian bargainers fully realize the breadth of the American proposals. The final agreement, reached two months later, was much more comprehensive than originally expected.

The proposals Finance Minister Fielding brought back from Washington in late January 1911 provided for free trade in most natural products and for reciprocal tariff reductions on a few selected manufactured items. Most Liberals were surprised and jubilant over what looked like a rare political plum. After four decades of fruitless requests for reciprocity, each rebuffed by Washington, not only had the Americans come to Ottawa on bended knee but a broad agreement for freer trade had actually

IMPRESSIONS OF LIFE IN LAURIER'S CANADA

For most Canadians, the closing years of the nineteenth century had been a decade of hard times. Now signs of change were everywhere; economic progress seemed to promise social advances and a future full of more hope than fear.

Some forty years after Confederation, Canada was a study in contrasts. Life in the growing industrial cities of Toronto and Winnipeg differed greatly from that in the Ontario countryside and rural Alberta. Changes were underway in traditional Canadian customs, clothing and lifestyles. The flurry of prosperity was producing an expanding middle class with more time for cultural pursuits, entertainment and community concerns.

This collage provides a glimpse of life, the arts and leisure in Laurier's Canada.

Gramophones were still something of a novelty in 1906 but were becoming more common every day.

Roy Beaver's Snake Show made the rounds of western agricultural fairs.

Wedding party, Keewatin, Ontario, 1910.

The Department of Health warned against buying ice cream from street vendors—without much success.

One of over 2000 people left homeless when fire destroyed 90 percent of the town of Windsor, Nova Scotia in 1897. Devastating fires swept through New Westminster, B.C., in 1898, Hull and Ottawa in 1900 and downtown Toronto in 1904.

Literary Landmarks

1897	W.H. Drummond, *The Habitant*
1897–1900	J. Castell Hopkins, ed., *Canada: An Encyclopedia*
1898	Ralph Connor, *Black Rock*
1899	Ralph Connor, *The Sky Pilot*
1900	Archibald Lampman, *Collected Poems*
1901	Ralph Connor, *The Man from Glengarry*
1905	W.H. Drummond, *The Voyageur*
1907	Robert Service, *Songs of A Sourdough* and *The Spell of the Yukon*
1908	Lucy Maude Montgomery, *Anne of Green Gables* Nellie McClung, *Sowing Seeds in Danny* Stephen Leacock, *Literary Lapses*
1911	Stephen Leacock, *Nonsense Novels* Pauline Johnson, *Legends of Vancouver*

Best remembered today as a determined and effective leader of the women's suffrage movement in the West, Nellie McClung first attracted the country's attention in 1908 with the publication of her very popular novel Sowing Seeds in Danny.

On warm summer Sundays, special excursion trains carried flocks of Winnipegers to the beaches on Lake Winnipeg.

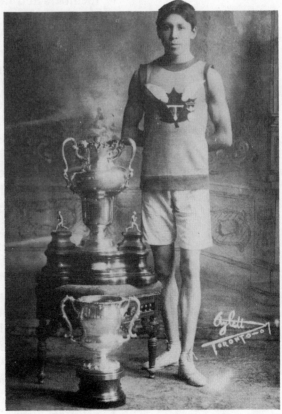

Tom Longboat won the Boston Marathon in 1907 and for the next few years was recognized as the best long-distance runner in America.

Anti-reciprocity cartoon

been concluded. It was, in the words of one observer, "the treaty of 1854 over again."

For their part, the Conservatives were thunderstruck. Even Tory leader Robert Borden conceded that the announcement of the proposals caused "the deepest dejection" among his party members and raised fears that the agreement would appeal to the voters and give Laurier's government another term of office.

But all was not lost. While the reciprocity proposals were approved by a special session of the American Congress in July 1911, they ran into considerable difficulty in Canada. The initial enthusiasm for the agreement expressed by western Conservatives and by many newspapers, including the *Toronto News* and the *Ottawa Journal*, soon dissipated. Strong and vociferous opposition surfaced in the ranks of both Laurier's Liberals and Borden's Conservatives. Reciprocity, according to critics, was really a frontal assault on the British connection, the "thin edge of the wedge" that would result in commercial and eventual political union with the United States.

Canadian anxieties over reciprocity were fanned by inflammatory rhetoric in the United States. Champ Clark, the Speaker of the House of Representatives, created an uproar in Canada with a remark made during the debate on the reciprocity proposals. "I am for the bill," he declared, "because I hope to see the day when the American flag will fly over every square foot of the British North American possessions clear to the North Pole." And even the American president, William Taft, in attempting to repudiate Clark's remark, added fuel to the fire by suggesting that Canada was now "at the parting of the ways." Such statements gave credence to wild claims that Canada faced a critical choice between "the British connection" and "American continentalism."

The Anti-Reciprocity Campaign

Much of the organized opposition to reciprocity came from the business, financial and manufacturing communities in Toronto and Montreal. After almost fifteen years of close co-operation with Laurier, business interests found that his government was no longer in their pocket. In the vanguard of the mounting wave of resistance to reciprocity was a group of eighteen Toronto Liberals, dubbed "The Toronto Eighteen," led by Sir Edmund Walker, President of the Canadian Bank of Commerce, and Zebulon A. Lash, a leading Toronto corporate lawyer. In February 1911 this group issued a strongly worded manifesto opposing the agreement and calling upon the country to block its approval. Reciprocity, they claimed, would destroy the Canadian economy which had developed under the National Policy of tariff protection, weaken the ties that bound Canada to the Empire and lead inevitably to Canada's absorption into the United States. In spite of all the blustering about "Imperial Unity" and "Canadian nationality," Walker privately conceded to friends like Colonel Sam Hughes that his group's real concern was not imperial policy, but the effect of reciprocity on the "industrial interest" in Canada.

American Investment
In the years before 1914, American investment was already well established in the Dominion. Over the period 1897-1914, estimated direct U.S. investment had risen from $160 million to a high of $618 million.

In Montreal, a group of prominent businessmen led by metal products manufacturer H.K.S. Hemming launched a vigorous campaign aimed squarely at reciprocity and defending the old National Policy tariff. As the campaign developed, the powerful Canadian Manufacturers' Association hurriedly set up the Canadian Home Manufacturers' Association in Toronto with links in Winnipeg and Montreal. The CHMA served as a vehicle for collecting financial contributions and was the source of anti-reciprocity propaganda distributed by the Canadian National League, under the direction of Z.A. Lash. The League organized meetings, churned out pamphlets and issued press releases to some three hundred daily and weekly newspapers across Canada.

The Branch Plant Issue

The great paradox of the National Policy and its brand of economic nationalism was evident in the 1911 anti-reciprocity campaign. Leading businessmen and Conservative protectionists defended the National Policy, resisting free trade and closer commercial relations with the United States. Yet strangely enough, they also praised the tariff for inducing American business enterprise to jump the tariff wall and establish branch factories in Canada. In other words, opponents of reciprocity played both sides of the fence. "No truck or trade with the Yankees" was their rallying cry, but at the same time they opposed reciprocity because it threatened the economic development of Canada by curtailing the inflow of American capital and enterprise. The nor-

During the 1911 election campaign, the pro-Laurier Toronto *Star* filled its windows with food items purchased in Toronto and across the border in Buffalo. Its conclusion—reciprocity would mean lower prices and greatly benefit average Canadians.

mally sombre *Monetary Times* was most emphatic. "American Capital will cease to establish Branch Factories in Canada," it proclaimed in bold headlines, "if Reciprocity Agreement is Approved." Such appeals had a telling effect not only on the leading economic interests, but also on the swelling ranks of industrial workers concerned about protecting their jobs.

Federal Conservatives took heart from the success of the campaign and began to mount an attack of their own. They received a real boost from the open defection of prominent Liberals, including Clifford Sifton and the Toronto Eighteen. After resigning as Minister of the Interior over the 1905 Autonomy Bills, Sifton had continued to sit as a Liberal in the House of Commons. He had voiced his disapproval of the reciprocity agreement while the negotiations were in progress, and when Laurier refused to delay consideration of the agreement, he rose in the House and denounced the proposals. His speech provided the Opposition with a raft of anti-reciprocity arguments and revealed a gaping hole in the Liberal ranks.

The 1911 Election
Sifton's defection served as the catalyst for an alliance of convenience between Conservatives and Liberal dissidents. On March

PROTECTION PROGRESS AND PROSPERITY
NOT Reciprocity Retrogression and Ruin

STEADY WORK. HIGH WAGES AND GOOD FOOD
Not Unemployment. Starvation Wages and Soup Kitchens.

2.500.000 MEN OUT of WORK IN THE UNITED STATES MEANS POOR FOOD AND SOUP KITCHENS

IN CANADA THERE ARE NO IDLE WORKMEN.

ARTICLES PURCHASED BY THE NEWS IN BUFFALO AND IN TORONTO

TORONTO & TORONTO WORKMEN NOT BUFFALO & BUFFALO WORKMEN

VOTE AGAINST RECIPROCITY AND AGAINST LOW WAGES FOR THOUSANDS OF WORKMEN

1, 1911, Sifton, Lash, John Willison, editor of the Toronto *News*, and Lloyd Harris, the Liberal M.P. for Brantford, met privately with Conservative leader Robert Borden and laid down seven conditions under which they would co-operate with the Tories to oppose reciprocity and bring down the government. Somewhat to the surprise of the dissident Liberals, a deal was struck. The Conservative leader agreed to "use every possible endeavour" to honour their conditions and, in return, the Liberal conspirators pledged to throw themselves into the coming battle.

Buoyed by his success at wooing prominent Liberals, Borden resolved to force an election on the reciprocity issue. Instead of seizing the initiative, an aging and cautious Laurier dithered while anti-reciprocity sentiment was whipped up in the country. Finally, after adjourning the House for an Imperial Conference and resuming the session in late July, the prime minister gave in to break a Tory parliamentary logjam. A federal election was called for September 1911 to settle the question.

As the election campaign got underway, the odds still seemed to favour Laurier and his Liberal government. The reciprocity agreement was not without supporters, and many saw it as a fitting culmination to fifteen years of unprecedented prosperity. The Conservative opposition was beset by internal divisions. Robert

The Conservative Toronto *News* in turn filled *its* windows with food bought in Toronto and Buffalo (and with Union Jacks) but concluded that reciprocity would mean low wages, unemployment and ruin.

Borden, a solid and respectable Halifax lawyer, had presided over the fractious party since 1901 but he had barely survived a succession of challenges to his sober style of leadership. Divisions within the party between English- and French-speaking Conservatives had surfaced on the naval issue and forced the postponement of a potentially divisive 1910 party convention. Some party loyalists openly opposed Borden's alliance with dissident Grits and his efforts to find a way of working with Bourassa's *nationalistes*.

The State of Party Organization

The appearances of the Liberal and Conservative parties were outwardly deceiving. For a party with a revered national leader and all the power of federal patronage, the Liberals showed surprising signs of weakness. By 1911 Laurier seemed to have lost touch with the party and the country. Only one of the ministers from his 1896 "cabinet of all talents" remained—the durable W.S. Fielding. But he, like Laurier, was older now and losing his former effectiveness. Laurier's control over Quebec was threatened as a result of the naval issue, and in Ontario the Liberal organization was in tatters. Laurier's Ontario lieutenant, Sir Allen Aylesworth, was by now an old, almost deaf party war-horse who had long since lost his sway over the province. To make matters worse, Liberal support among the industrial class in Ontario's growing cities and towns had been eroded by popular fears that reciprocity would cause the closing of many factories.

Meanwhile, the Tories were closing ranks. Disputes at the top over leadership and parliamentary squabbling did not seem to reach the constituencies. In the absence of a strong national party structure, Borden's campaign relied heavily on the political machines of four provincial Tory Governments. The Conservative party apparatus in Ontario, where the crucial battle would be waged, had been transformed by Premier James P. Whitney from a feeble, skeletal organization in 1907 to a well-oiled political machine in 1911. In Manitoba and British Columbia, and to a lesser degree in New Brunswick, local organization had been solidified through close co-operation with the ruling provincial parties. This spirit of co-operation, together with the overflowing war chest provided by anti-reciprocity businessmen, made the Tories a force to be reckoned with in the 1911 contest.

An "Unholy Alliance"

While in English-speaking Canada the parties battled over reciprocity, in Quebec the contest turned mainly on the naval question. Here Robert Borden and the Conservatives tailored their platform to make it more palatable to Bourassa and the *nationalistes*. Borden's speeches attacked Laurier's naval policy, but discreetly said nothing of a financial contribution to the Royal

Opposite page:
Robert Borden had little of Laurier's charm or eloquence, but he was a man of intelligence, determination and unquestioned integrity.

Navy. At Borden's request, Quebec Conservative C.H. Cahan approached Bourassa, Armand Lavergne and other *nationalistes* and secured their co-operation against Laurier. This informal arrangement, labelled by Mackenzie King an "unholy alliance," seemed to do the trick. The federal Conservatives refrained from opposing *nationaliste* candidates wherever possible and the Conservative leader in the province, F.D. Monk, even campaigned as a self-proclaimed *nationaliste*.

On the eve of the election Sir Wilfrid seemed to sense defeat in the air. To stay in power, he had to maintain his political grip on Quebec, while taking care not to completely alienate Ontario and the rest of English Canada. In a stirring address at Saint John, Laurier made a final plea for his "policy of true Canadianism, of moderation, of conciliation." His eloquence fell largely on deaf ears in Quebec. To Bourassa's *nationalistes* and a growing number of French Canadians, he was a *vendu*, one who had sold out to the English. He seemed to take Quebec for granted while courting Ontario's affection. Laurier's brand of compromise seemed like a one-way street: only the French Canadians, following his noble leadership, were forced to compromise. The "sunny way" meant that French-speaking Canadians alone, and not *les Anglais*, had to sacrifice their interests for the sake of national unity.

The Verdict

On September 21, 1911, the people of Canada rendered their verdict. Sir Wilfrid Laurier, seventy years old and prime minister of Canada for fifteen years, was swept out of power. The scale of the election victory by Robert Borden and the Conservatives was amazing. Borden's Conservatives captured 134 seats, compared to only 87 for the Liberals. In Quebec the Bourassa-Monk alliance took 27 of 65 seats, for a gain of 16. In Ontario the Liberals were smashed by a Conservative machine which gained 32 seats, taking 72 of the province's 86. These breakthroughs were matched by similar triumphs in British Columbia and the Maritimes. Only on the prairies did the Liberals hold their own. The Laurier years were over.

The Laurier Legacy

Looking back from 1911, Canadians could have been struck by how much their country had changed during the Laurier years. The Dominion's population had jumped from five to seven and a quarter million people, and two new prairie provinces had been added to Confederation. The prairie West had been filled by thousands of agricultural pioneers and transformed into the new "Granary of the Empire." Shifts in population and the inflow of immigrants were creating a new, more urbanized Canada. In central Canada the rise of modern industrialism was drawing men

"I am branded in Quebec as a traitor to the French, and in Ontario as a traitor to the English. In Quebec I am branded as a Jingoist, and in Ontario as a separatist. In Quebec I am attacked as an Imperialist, and in Ontario as an anti-Imperialist. I am neither. I am a Canadian."

Sir Wilfrid Laurier in a 1911 campaign speech

and women to the cities from the farm and from overseas. Among the growing Canadian population was a new element, the "foreigners," struggling to make a home and gain acceptance in Canadian society. New cities and towns had sprung up in the West and elsewhere, new railways and booming factories had been built, and new roads were now used by new-fangled automobiles.

The Laurier years had been a time of bright promise and unparalleled prosperity. A modern, industrialized Canada was taking shape. Yet the wealth, vulgar materialism and stark inequalities of the period had produced a rising chorus of criticism. Western farm and labour leaders complained that their followers had not received their fair share of the economic pie. French-Canadian *nationalistes* had grown fearful that their cultural identity was being eroded by the rush to industrialism. Social reformers of all political stripes had raised concerns about city slums, civic sanitation, women's rights and temperance, all issues associated with an emerging urban industrial society. In intellectual and cultural roles, groups of Canadian imperial-nationalists had emerged demanding programs to "Canadianize" the recent immigrants. In each case, the critics seemed to be urging new public policies and programs to help ease the transition from an agricultural to an industrial society.

Sir Wilfrid Laurier retained his seat in Parliament and remained leader of the opposition until his death on February 17, 1919.

By 1911 Wilfrid Laurier seemed to have lost touch with Canada. As prime minister from 1896 to 1911, he held to a nineteenth-century brand of Liberalism, a philosophy which was overtaken by the changes in Canadian society. Toward the end of his time in office, Laurier had begun to sense the need for new public policies. But the only new policy he could offer was reciprocity, a popular trade arrangement from the past.

A new industrial society demanded new approaches to government. The seeds of Laurier's downfall lay in his inability to adapt his liberal philosophy to the needs of modern industrial Canada. Toronto newspaper editor John Willison observed in 1911 that Laurier was classed in Canada as a Liberal, but that in England his policies would have been "considered as strongly Conservative." It was this brand of *laissez-faire* liberalism which prevented him from meeting public demands for "interventionist" government in a new, industrial Canada.

Sir Wilfrid's fall from grace brought an abrupt end to fifteen years of Liberal ascendancy in Ottawa. A new political cycle was beginning under the energetic new government of Robert Borden and the Conservatives. Yet many Canadians shared a sense of loss. Wilfrid Laurier, depicted by his official biographer, O.D. Skelton, as a heroic "Sir Galahad," seemed to symbolize purity, eloquence and harmony between Canada's two founding peoples. Now he was gone. The Liberal mythology had been shattered and the promise of Laurier Liberalism left largely unfulfilled.

REVIEW AND DISCUSSION

Key People and Ideas

Explain the importance of each of the following as they are discussed in the chapter.

Armand Lavergne
Andrew Macphail
Charles Mair
Sir Frederick Borden
Robert Borden
Champ Clark
Sir Edmund Walker
"The Toronto Eighteen"
F.D. Monk

HMS *Dreadnought*
Naval Service Bill
Le Devoir
Boundary Waters Treaty
International Joint Commission
Department of External Affairs
Reciprocity
Canadian Home Manufacturer's
 Association
The "Unholy Alliance"

Analysing the Issues

Answer each of the following questions, which deal with important issues raised in the chapter.

1. What were the conflicting perceptions of Canada's interests through which Laurier tried to steer a middle course?
2. What military reforms did the Laurier government initiate in the cause of asserting Canada's independence from Great Britain?
3. How did Laurier's policy on naval defence lead to an alliance between Borden and Bourassa?
4. What factors led Laurier to support the idea of reciprocity with the United States?
5. What factors led to Laurier's defeat in the election of 1911?

Question for Discussion

Think carefully about the following question and discuss the issues it raises.

1. Make a chart comparing Wilfrid Laurier's strengths and weaknesses as prime minister of Canada. Pay particular attention to Laurier's policy of compromise on issues of French–English relations, his aggressive policies to encourage immigration, and his *laissez-faire* approach to the development of the Canadian economy. On balance, how do you rate Laurier as prime minister? Justify your view, using evidence from your chart.

Further Reading

No period of modern Canadian history has been subjected to more study than the Laurier era. Listed here are some of the best and most reliable books dealing with the period, but remember that no historian knows the whole story.

General Overviews

- Brown, R.C. and Ramsay Cook. *Canada 1896–1921: A Nation Transformed.* Toronto: McClelland and Stewart, 1974. A fine, scholarly survey of the Laurier–Borden years, now recognized as the standard work on the period.
- Clippingdale, Richard. *Laurier: His Life and His World.* Toronto: McGraw-Hill Ryerson, 1979. A handsome, polished study of Laurier, treating the man within the social and political context of his time.
- Phillips, Alan. *Into the 20th Century, 1900–1910.* Toronto: Canada's Illustrated Heritage Series, 1977. A profusely illustrated popular social history of Canada in the first decade of the new century.
- Spigelman, Martin. *Wilfrid Laurier.* Don Mills: Fitzhenry and Whiteside, 1978. A brief, readable biography, focusing heavily on political events but offering some critical perspectives on Laurier.

Special Studies

- Berger, Carl, ed. *Imperialism and Nationalism, 1884–1914: A Conflict in Canadian Thought.* Toronto: Copp Clark, 1969. A first rate collection of viewpoints and interpretations on imperialism and nationalism in the 1884–1914 period.
- Bliss, Michael. *A Living Profit: Studies in the Social History of Canadian Business, 1883–1911.* McClelland and Stewart, 1974. A thoughtful, wide-ranging study of Canadian businessmen and their attitudes toward tariffs, competition and labour in the period.
- Bruce, Jean. *The Last Best West.* Toronto: Fitzhenry and Whiteside, 1976. One of the best illustrated histories of the Canadian West in its formative years. Revealing photos accompanied by fascinating documentary commentaries.
- Gray, James. *Boomtime: Peopling the Canadian Prairies.* Saskatoon: Western Producer Books, 1979. A highly personal pictorial account of the settlement of the prairie West by one of Canada's greatest storytellers.
- Kealey, Linda, ed. *A Not Unreasonable Claim: Women and Reform in Canada 1880s–1920s.* Toronto: The Women's Press, 1979. A collection of provocative essays on women's participation in social reform movements.
- Levitt, Joseph, ed. *Henri Bourassa on Imperialism and Biculturalism.* Toronto: Copp Clark, 1970. A sourcebook of documents and short readings concerning Henri Bourassa and the imperial question.
- Piva, Michael J. *The Condition of the Working Class in Toronto: 1900–1921.* Ottawa: University of Ottawa Press, 1979. A thorough, detailed study of working class conditions in Toronto, focusing on health, housing and labour conflict in the Laurier years.
- Rasmussen, Linda et al. *A Harvest Yet to Reap: A History of Prairie Women.* Toronto: The Women's Press, 1976. The story of western women, told through a collection of photographs, letters and newspaper items.
- Stevens, Paul, ed. *The General Election of 1911: A Study in Canadian Politics.* Toronto: Copp Clark, 1970. A fascinating collection of documents and analyses of the 1911 election which ended the Laurier era.

Index

Page numbers in italics refer to illustrations, captions and/or margin notes.